1 JOHN: RELYING ON THE LOVE OF GOD

Scotty Smith

STUDY GUIDE WITH LEADER'S NOTES

New
Growth
Press
newgrowthpress.com

New Growth Press, Greensboro, NC 27401
newgrowthpress.com
Copyright © 2021 by Scotty Smith

Unless otherwise indicated, Scripture quotations are taken from The Holy Bible, New International Version˚, NIV˚. Copyright © 1973, 1978, 1984, 2011 by Biblica, Inc.˚ Used by permission. All rights reserved worldwide.

Scripture quotations marked (ESV) are from The ESV˚ Bible (The Holy Bible, English Standard Version˚), copyright © 2001 by Crossway, a publishing ministry of Good News Publishers. Used by permission. All rights reserved.

Cover Design: Faceout Books, faceoutstudio.com
Interior Design and Typesetting: Gretchen Logterman
Exercises and Application Questions: Jack Klumpenhower

ISBN: 978-1-64507-186-0 (Print)
ISBN: 978-1-64507-187-7 (eBook)

Printed in India

29 28 27 26 25 24 23 22   3 4 5 6 7

CONTENTS

INTRODUCTION

If the apostle John had been an Old Testament psalm writer, we might easily imagine him composing this ode to the love of God and the God of love: "Because your love is better than life, my lips will glorify you" (Psalm 63:3). John's New Testament writings—his gospel, three epistles, and the book of Revelation—aren't just a storehouse of rich theology. They are a theater in which we see John coming alive to the only love better than life, the love God lavishes on us in Jesus.

It's not just what John says that grabs us; it's how the truth grabbed John that intrigues us. Many vignettes in his story endear John to us. He was the disciple who leaned against Jesus at the Last Supper. He was the one to whom Jesus, from the cross, committed the care of his mother. On the morning of Jesus's resurrection, John outran Peter to the empty tomb, saw evidence of the resurrection, and believed.

John referred to himself as the disciple Jesus loved. Surely, this was not because John felt Jesus loved him more than the others, but because John treasured the love of Jesus so deeply. We identify ourselves by the things we treasure. They become the things that most define us. For John, nothing defined him more than the love God has for us in Jesus.

By studying 1 John, you are stepping into that same experience. John wants nothing less for his readers than for them to be defined by the love of God. As with all the small-group resources in this

1

series, this study guide is written to keep you looking at God's love for you in Christ. John's purpose in writing will be met if you too come to see yourself first of all as someone intensely, astonishingly loved by Jesus.

HOW TO USE THIS STUDY

This guide will help you do this in a group study. John wrote his letter not to a single believer, but to an entire church family. It is meant to be studied alongside other believers. Doing this lets you benefit from what God is also teaching them, and it gives you their encouragement as you apply what you learn.

In his letter, John insists that believers be people who admit their sin as they grow in confidence that Jesus saves them from that sin. Therefore, this study guide will encourage you not to gloss over your sins and struggles. It will ask you to share both deep needs and deep hopes. Expect differences in how people participate. It's okay if some in the group are eager to share right away while others take it slowly, or if some find 1 John cheerful while others are troubled. But because John is training us to "know and rely on the love God has for us" (1 John 4:16), also expect to be drawn closer to Jesus. Expect your time in 1 John to change those in your group—starting with you!

Each participant should have one of these study guides in order to join in reading and be able to work through the exercises during that part of the study. The study leader should read through both the lesson and the leader's notes in the back of this book before each lesson begins. Otherwise, no preparation or homework is required from any participant.

There are eight lessons in this study guide. Each lesson will take about an hour to complete, perhaps a bit more if your group is large, and will include these elements:

BIG IDEA. This is a summary of the main point of the lesson.

BIBLE CONVERSATION. Your group will read a passage from 1 John and discuss it. As the heading suggests, the Bible conversation questions are intended to spark a conversation rather than generate correct answers. In most cases, the questions will have several possible good answers. The leader's notes at the back of this book provide some insights, but don't just turn there for the "right answer." At times, the group may want to see what the notes say, but always try to answer for yourselves first by thinking about the Bible passage.

ARTICLE. This is the main teaching section of the lesson, written by the book's author.

DISCUSSION. The discussion questions following the article will help you apply the teaching to your life. Again, there will be several good ways to answer each question.

EXERCISE. The exercise is a section you will complete on your own during group time. You can write in the book if that helps you, or you can just think about your responses. You will then share some of what you learned with the group. If the group is large, it may help to split up to share the results of the exercise and to pray, so that everyone has a better opportunity to participate.

WRAP-UP AND PRAYER. Prayer is a critical part of the lesson because your spiritual growth will happen through God's work in you, not by your self-effort. Your group will be asking him to do that good work.

By studying 1 John, you are about to encounter both John's authoritative truth and his transformative experience. Writing to friends under duress, John boldly declares, "God is love." This is profound theology, indeed. But it is also an open invitation to have that truth redefine you. John bids you, "See what great love the Father has lavished on us, that we should be called children of God! And that is what we are!" (1 John 3:1).

1

MADE FOR INTIMACY WITH GOD

BIG IDEA

God created and redeemed us for a rich, joyful relationship with himself and his Son, Jesus.

BIBLE CONVERSATION *20 MINUTES*

The readers of John's epistle—believers in Asia Minor (modern-day Turkey) near the end of the first century—were facing challenges that would require a greater reliance on God and his love than they had even known. They were under assault, externally and internally.

External assault. Persecution of Christians was becoming systematic. As a faithful pastor, John worked to prepare his beloved friends for life in an increasingly hostile world. Quite probably, within a few years John himself was arrested by the Roman government and sent into exile on the island of Patmos, where the aging apostle would write the book of Revelation.

Internal assault. False teachers had infiltrated the church, seeking to combine elements of Gnosticism with Christian spirituality. Gnosticism taught that physical matter is evil and only immaterial spirit should be celebrated as real, valuable, and lasting. The Gnostics spoke of God as existing above the molecules and messes of the world and known only by initiates who acquire special knowledge (*gnosis*) which transports the soul closer to God through multi-layered tiers of heaven. This meant that for Gnostics, salvation was achieved by knowledge, not received by grace. They viewed distance, not their sinful depravity, as their biggest obstacle to knowing God. They championed personal enlightenment, not transformation into Jesus's image. They sought freedom through celestial transcendence, not heartfelt repentance. But any addition to the gospel is always a subtraction. By rejecting a physical Savior and downplaying sin, these false teachers denied the reality of Jesus's incarnation, his substitutionary death for sin on the cross, and his bodily resurrection. Take these away, and you gut the gospel.

With this background in mind, have someone read **1 John 1:1–4** aloud. Then discuss the questions below.

Look closely at how John describes the Word of life, Jesus. How is John's description of Jesus better than what the Gnostics imagined? How is it better than many people today imagine?

John describes eternal life as "fellowship" both with God and with each other. The original Greek word is *koinonia*, which also can describe intimacy between spouses. How is this different, and better, than the way you might describe eternal life if you were asked about it?

John says his reason for writing is "to make our [or your] joy complete." Why is joy important in the life of a believer?

✶✶✶✶✶

Now read the following article by this book's author. Have participants take turns reading it aloud, switching readers at each paragraph break.

THE MESSAGE OF 1 JOHN

5 MINUTES

I haven't always read 1 John through the lens of the gospel. My first introduction to this epistle was on a retreat led by some rather zealous believers. Looking back, I can see that they were clearly more familiar with God's law than with his grace. It was on one of those make-Jesus-Lord-of your-life kinds of weekends.

If those guys were writing this study guide, they would probably want to title it something like *The Marks of a REAL Believer*, or *God's Scorecard: What He's Looking for in Your Life*, or *Discipleship for the Serious, Not the Slackers*. It's possible to read any book in the Bible and miss or marginalize Jesus. It's possible, but destructive. We don't make Jesus Lord of anything. We acknowledge his lordship over everything and live accordingly, with humility and joy.

First John certainly highlights key fruit the gospel will bear in our lives—but that's the point. It's the gospel, not us, that produces the fruit. The apostle Paul put it this way: "The gospel is bearing fruit and growing throughout the whole world—just as it has been doing among you since the day you heard it and truly understood

God's grace" (Colossians 1:6). We are to grow in grace, by grace. Fruit that lasts will be produced by the Holy Spirit.

John's letter begins with a doxological burst of bold affirmations. Every phrase is meant to sabotage the false teaching gaining headway among believers in Asia Minor. Notice John's calculated reference to creation, "the beginning." It echoes both the first verse of Genesis and John's opening line in his gospel. Matter matters, because God created all things through Jesus. Consider also John's multiple-sensory experience of Jesus: hearing, seeing, touching "with our own hands."

The false teachers weren't entirely wrong. *Gnosis* ("knowledge") does save. But it is not gaining some hidden and mystical knowledge; it is knowing an unquestionably human, delightfully relatable person.

Jesus came from the Father into a real world. Gnosticism supposed that we should go up into an immaterial realm to find God. John proclaims that God came down to us in the person of Jesus Christ. The gospel is about an actual person, not a philosophical phantom. Jesus isn't a grand idea, but a great Savior. He came to us that we might share in the wonder and riches of eternal life.

God created us for a robust, deeply satisfying intimacy with himself—a relational richness that has implications for every aspect of our lives. The storyboard for this relationship is a real world of geography, flora, and fauna. The garden of Eden was the first chapter in this grand story. The new heaven and new earth, the ultimate garden city, will be its finale and fullness.

In between the two, the Bible reveals the tragic saga of our sin and brokenness, and the unfolding wonder of God's commitment to redeem and restore. As great as our sin is, God's love for his broken image-bearers is thousands of times greater. By his grace,

God is calling a family into relationship with himself from every nation, tribe, people, and language. And by his grace, he enables his children to know him better and better.

What, then, is my summary of the message of 1 John? I don't want to miss Jesus like that retreat in my youth did, so my summary flows from two key gospel truths:

First, knowing God, not living forever, is how the Bible defines eternal life. In his gospel, John recorded Jesus's own definition of eternal life. "Now this is eternal life: that they know you, the only true God, and Jesus Christ, whom you have sent" (John 17:3). That we will live forever is wonderful. But that we will grow in our relationship with our Father and with Jesus, whom we too will one day be able to see and touch, is unparalleled awesomeness.

Second, relying on God, not our own achievements, is our source of eternal life. God's zeal to be known is powerfully captured by the prophet Jeremiah: "Let not the wise man boast in his wisdom, let not the mighty man boast in his might, let not the rich man boast in his riches, but let him who boasts boast in this, that he understands and knows me" (Jeremiah 9:23–24 esv). This is the Father who made us and is pursuing us. He delights for us to boast in him. In the Scriptures, our "boast" isn't our brag; it's what we rely on for salvation, both temporal and eternal. Because we are riddled with unbelief and addicted to self-sufficiency, we will be in the learning-to-rely school until heaven.

Knowing and relying on the love of God. That is as good of a summary of 1 John as I can offer, because it is taken from John's own words: "And so we know and rely on the love God has for us. God is love. Whoever lives in love lives in God, and God in them" (1 John 4:16–17). These words are crammed full of mystery, goodness, and invitation. First John is dedicated to unpacking the mystery, heralding the goodness, and extending the invitation to a greater knowledge of God and his reliance-worthy love.

This is a life of grace from beginning to end. As John's friends needed to know, God's grace is sufficient for every context, contest, and crucible of life. This isn't religious cliché, a pious muse, or sentimental spirituality. At times, it is a matter of life and death. First John won't just show us the greatness of the love of God, but also how it is essential. Oxygen isn't just nice; it's necessary. It's the same with the love of God, lavished on us in the gospel.

DISCUSSION *10 MINUTES*

For their salvation, the Gnostics relied on achieving a higher level of knowledge. What personal achievements are believers today tempted to rely on instead of solely trusting Jesus for salvation? Why is trust in these achievements so enticing?

What about spiritual growth? What personal achievements are you tempted to rely on for your spiritual growth instead of relying on the Holy Spirit? Explain why, if you can.

TOO-SMALL IMPRESSIONS OF ETERNAL LIFE

20 MINUTES

You probably have some impressions about eternal life that fall short of what the Bible says. Perhaps you got these impressions from popular culture, or even from Christian culture. You might realize or suspect that these ideas are wrong, but they still affect how you react to the idea of eternal life.

A fuller sense of the wonder of eternal life can bolster your hope in Jesus. So for this exercise, consider some of the too-small impressions of eternal life that creep into your thinking. Begin by working on your own. Read through the descriptions of how eternal life is more than we sometimes think. Note some ways you most want to grow in your appreciation of eternal life, and complete the sentence at the end. When the group is ready, you'll have a chance to discuss your responses.

I want to better appreciate how eternal life is . . .

☐ **More than CLOUDS AND HARPS.** Eternal life is not just a *place* of ease and visual beauty, but a *person* of warmth and relational beauty. "We will be with the Lord forever" (1 Thessalonians 4:17).

☐ **More than an ENDLESS TIME LOOP.** Eternal life is not just living forever, but a lavish life jammed full of fellowship with Jesus. "I desire to depart and be with Christ, which is better by far" (Philippians 1:23).

☐ **More than COFFEE WITH A FRIEND.** This fellowship with Jesus is not just casual enjoyment, but deep intimacy with a perfect lover. Notice how *koinonia* is also how John describes the eternal intimacy between the Father, Son, and Holy Spirit.

☐ **More than JESUS-AND-ME TIME.** This *koinonia* is not just private time with Jesus, but perfect fellowship and feasting with each other too. "The LORD Almighty will prepare a feast of rich food for all peoples" (Isaiah 25:6).

☐ **More than a CRUISE-SHIP LIFE.** Eternal life is not just an end to suffering with all needs catered to, but complete joy. In John's gospel, he notes that when Jesus prayed for his disciples the night before he died, he prayed "that they may have the full measure of my joy within them" (John 17:13).

☐ **More than a GHOSTLY EXISTENCE.** Eternal life is not just a spiritual presence, but a firmly physical life with Jesus when he returns. "After my skin has been destroyed, yet in my flesh I will see God" (Job 19:26).

☐ **More than a TRANSPORTER-BEAM DESTINATION.** Eternal life is not just an instant escape from our physical world. Rather, it is the entire, vigorous experience of the created world we were made to enjoy and will enjoy when Jesus returns. "Creation itself will be liberated from its bondage to decay and brought into the freedom and glory of the children of God" (Romans 8:21).

❒ **More than a DISTANT DREAM.** Eternal life is not just coming one day, but begins now. Notice how John uses present tense: "Our fellowship is with the Father and with the Son." The *koinonia* that will soon be perfect is already a treasure today.

❒ **More than a GOLD MEDAL.** Eternal life is not an achievement to earn, meant to pressure you now, but a gift of grace meant to delight you now and forever. Although you do run hard because you see the prize that awaits, it is all "by faith in the Son of God, who loved me and gave himself for me" (Galatians 2:20).

❒ **More than** _____. (Pick your own that's true of you.)

One truth about eternal life that would give me greater hope in Jesus if I more often remembered and believed it is _____ _____.

When the group is ready, share some of your responses. What too-small impressions of eternal life are sometimes part of your thinking? What bigger and better truths about eternal life do you most want to learn, and why?

If you more often remembered and believed these truths about eternal life, how might the way you live for Jesus today change? Try to be specific.

WRAP-UP AND PRAYER *10 MINUTES*

Remember that John says his purpose in writing his epistle is to increase joy. As part of your closing prayer time, pray together that the Holy Spirit would use his words, spoken to you through 1 John, to increase your joy in Jesus as you complete this study.

2

JESUS'S LIFE FOR US AND IN US

BIG IDEA

Knowing Jesus informs our minds, enflames our hearts, and changes our lives.

BIBLE CONVERSATION *20 MINUTES*

The false teachers John confronts in his letter made a too-sharp distinction between their thinking, spiritual lives and their doing, physical lives. This resulted in two gospel-denying errors about themselves: (1) they trusted their own achievement of superior knowledge and inner discovery instead of trusting Christ, and (2) they downplayed their sinful acts to the point where they lost any sense of their need for a Savior and the forgiveness and transformation he brings.

With these errors in mind, John presents the true gospel in **1 John 1:5–2:6**. Have someone read that passage aloud. Then discuss the questions below.

In verses 5–7, John uses the word *light* to describe God and life with him. What about God and the Christian life makes "light" a fitting description? Think of several good answers.

Which parts of this passage comfort you, and which make you uncomfortable? Explain why.

Verse 9 affirms both Jesus's completed work *for us* (our sins are forgiven) and his ongoing work *in us* (he is making us pure). Does your view of your life in Christ include both of these, or do you tend to focus mostly on one? Explain.

✶✶✶✶✶

Now take turns reading the article aloud, switching readers at each paragraph break. When you finish, discuss the questions that follow the article.

THE LYRIC AND MUSIC OF THE GOSPEL

5 MINUTES

I greatly love Christmas carols and the hymns of Advent. In fact, I've been listening to many of them as I've been writing this study. They tell the unfolding story of redemption with poetry and joyful passion. And they always direct our heart-gaze to Jesus as the point, hero, and worship-worthy one. Their lyrics and melodies anchor the gospel in our bones.

I know John didn't have any of our hymns and carols, but he certainly modeled what it means to live with a ferocious commitment to good theology and an uninhibited love for Jesus. Two Advent hymns, in particular, have been on the playlist of my heart as I've been studying 1 John. They capture the central themes of John's letter. The first is "Hark, the Herald Angels Sing," written by Charles Wesley. I especially love the third verse:

> Hail the heav'n-born Prince of Peace!
> Hail the Sun of Righteousness!
> Light and life to all he brings,
> Ris'n with healing in his wings.
> Mild he lays his glory by,

> Born that we no more may die,
> Born to raise us from the earth,
> Born to give us second birth.

"Mild." Humbly, with no fanfare, Jesus laid aside his glory—though he never ceased to be God. John zealously defends the incarnation in his letter. Why? Because our need is so great that only God can save us. We need resurrection, not a redo. We need a life-substitute, not a life coach. We need a God who came to find us, not a way to find God within ourselves.

"Light and life." Jesus gives light to us, and not merely as a candle for our path. It's more like he opens the lid on our casket. Only the great light of Jesus can dispel the deep darkness of our lives and of our world. Light is a major theme in John's writings. This isn't light for private illumination, as the false teachers taught, but the light of Jesus who reveals the glory of God and the darkness of our need. God does for us what we could never do for ourselves: he delivers us from Satan's dark dominion and places us in the kingdom of his beloved Son.

"Prince of Peace and Sun of Righteousness." Jesus gives us peace with God because, by his righteousness, he fulfilled the demands God's law and took the judgment for our unrighteousness. This is why John can confidently declare that God is being just when he forgives us (v. 9). Since Jesus fully met the demands of righteousness, God would be unjust not to save those who trust in Jesus. We are comprehensively forgiven and declared righteous by God.

"Risen with healing." As the rising sun gives warmth and health, Jesus rose from the dead so that aspect of our being is marked for healing—body, soul, and spirit. This whole-person salvation is the gospel John proclaims and defends. Jesus wasn't born to give us a second chance, but a second birth. Because Jesus died, we won't. Because Jesus was raised, we shall be also. Because Jesus is coming back, we will be made like him. How pure are we destined to become? As lovely and loving as Jesus.

"Hail." We hail Jesus as an act of honor and humble gratitude. The unabashed adoration of Jesus permeates all five chapters of John's letter. Every line of woo, woe, and well-being in 1 John bids us worship Jesus.

The second Advent hymn I've been humming while studying 1 John is "Joy to the World" written by Isaac Watts. Like John's letter, it broadens our understanding of Jesus's work to include every sphere of life and every corner of the cosmos: "He comes to make his blessings flow far as the curse is found." The false teachers thought only of salvation for the inner person, but John worshiped a Savior whose redemptive work flows to every place sin and death have done their destructive work. Jesus is making all things new.

> He rules the world with truth and grace,
> and makes the nations prove
> the glories of his righteousness
> and wonders of his love.

Jesus's relationship to the physical world is both heart-encouraging and mission-fueling. He is presently ruling the world of nature, nations, neighborhoods, and nanoseconds by his truth and grace. Jesus hasn't come to annihilate or replace the created universe, but to restore it. John lived in light of God's covenant commitment to redeem a family of believers from every race, tribe, tongue, and people group. The nations are proving, and will prove, the glories of Jesus's righteousness and the wonders of his love, as the gospel runs to the ends of the earth.

How are we to understand John's desire for believers not to sin? I believe John is both giving an exhortation and expressing hope. We don't have sinless perfection yet, but John has a view to the day when believers *will* be completely sin-free. The Father has begun a work in us, and in the world, which he will complete. Sinlessness *is* in our future. Hallelujah! One day, we will not sin in thought, word, or deed—ever again. Pause for a moment and drink that in. It almost seems too good to be true.

DISCUSSION *10 MINUTES*

The article mentions several events in the story of redemption: Jesus's birth, his God-revealing life, his death for sin, his resurrection, his mission to the nations, and his plan to make all things new. Which of these would you like to appreciate better so that Jesus becomes a bigger hero to you? Explain.

What role does joyful passion have in your life with Jesus? How do you express it?

Lesson

EXERCISE

2

LAW, ANTI-LAW, AND GOSPEL

20 MINUTES

The two great distortions of the gospel presented at the beginning of this lesson have appeared throughout church history and are still with us today. We can think of them as *law* and *anti-law*:

Law (often called legalism): You rely on your obedience. You feel you must suppress the appetites and desires of your body through rigorous spiritual discipline, gaining and maintaining God's favor by your human effort. Jesus is more a model to follow than a Savior to trust. This may lead to arrogant pride if you think you are successful or to despair and endless worry if you realize you are not.

Anti-law (often called antinomianism): You don't take obedience seriously. You feel you may indulge in the appetites and desires of your body because you are now "under grace" and God's law doesn't matter much. Jesus is more a get-out-of-hell token than a whole-life Savior who renews everything—including your behavior. The hallmark of this error is an attitude that presumes on God's favor.

For this exercise, begin by working on your own. Read some verses from our passage in 1 John. Also read the law or anti-law ways people might react to those verses, and the gospel response that's better. Finish by noting which of the law and anti-law distortions you have seen in others or in yourself. The distortions are numbered to help you refer to them easily. When the group is ready, you'll share some of your results and discuss the gospel responses.

"If we claim to be without sin, we deceive ourselves and the truth is not in us" (1 John 1:8).

(1) Law distortion: "My sin usually doesn't include any real whoppers. I'm doing pretty well compared to most people—I hope."

(2) Anti-law distortion: "I prefer not to think of it as sin, which sounds too accusing and condemning. I just need to learn more and grow in spiritual enlightenment."

Gospel: "I need a big rescue. I need more than a little enlightenment; I need a resurrection from my deadness. That means both forgiveness for my rebellion against Jesus and renewal to become like Jesus—a need so great only Jesus himself can meet it."

"If we confess our sins, he is faithful and just and will forgive us our sins and purify us from all unrighteousness" (1:9).

(3) Law distortion: "I need to make sure I confess. I better not miss any sins, or God might not forgive those."

(4) Anti-law distortion: "Of course God forgives. He's supposed to. He's merciful."

Gospel: "I know I'm forgiven not merely because I hope God is merciful, but because I'm sure he is just. He would not punish me when he's already punished Jesus in my place. So I gladly confess my sin as a habit of ongoing faith, agreeing with my Father that I have wronged him but he counts me right in Christ."

"I write this so that you will not sin. But if anybody does sin, we have an advocate with the Father—Jesus Christ, the Righteous One. He is the atoning sacrifice for our sins" (2:1–2).

(5) Law distortion: "I must try harder and do better so Jesus won't stop advocating for me. Maybe if I pick some outward rules and keep those, it will prove to Jesus that I'm trying."

(6) Anti-law distortion: "I have an advocate who sacrificed himself for my sin. So now it doesn't really matter anymore if I sin or not. I can do whatever I want."

Gospel: "Sin kills. It's ugly and self-sabotaging. I love Jesus, so I hate sin. Yet when I do sin, I don't despair because I have an advocate in heaven today, and because I look in hope to the future when 'you will not sin' will be fully true of me."

"Whoever says, 'I know him,' but does not do what he commands is a liar, and the truth is not in that person" (2:4).

(7) Law distortion: "Oh, no! I need to earn my way into Jesus by living the way Jesus lived. It sounds awfully hard. That verse condemns me."

(8) Anti-law distortion: "I'm going to pretend that verse isn't there. God is all about grace."

Gospel: "Obeying God is hard, but I can see how my love for Jesus will show up in how I live the way he lived. In Jesus, God's law no longer condemns me nor puts endless pressure on me to perform. This frees my obedience to be a true delight—and validation that I am in Jesus and he is working in me."

Now, for each statement below, pick one of the law or anti-law distortions above to complete the statement.

- _____ is a mind-set or belief I have often seen in others.

- _____ is a mind-set or belief I used to hold.

- Although I know better, _____ is still a feeling I get or is my gut-level reaction to these verses.

When the group is ready, share some of your results. What are the law or anti-law distortions you've seen in others or in yourself? Do you notice any patterns?

What gospel responses do you want to learn and embrace? How might doing so change your outlook on life, your work for Christ's kingdom, or your relationship with your heavenly Father?

WRAP-UP AND PRAYER *10 MINUTES*

As part of your prayer time together, be sure to pray about the gospel responses you want to learn to embrace. Ask your Father to teach them to you and to use them in you, so that you have a Christ-led life.

Lesson

3

LIVING AS CHILDREN OF LIGHT

BIG IDEA

We are to love each other as Jesus loves us, wherever God has placed us in his world.

BIBLE CONVERSATION *20 MINUTES*

Having said that anyone who claims to live in Jesus must live the way Jesus did, John goes on to explain in **John 2:7–17** this will be a life of love. The passage includes lines addressed to fathers, young men, and children. John's purpose is not to neglect mothers and young women, but to emphasize all ages and stages of growth in the family of God (note that elsewhere he uses feminine terms to refer to God's people collectively—see 2 John 1). The point is that all of us, young and old, male and female, are saved by the same grace and called to grow in love until Jesus returns.

Have someone read the passage aloud. Then discuss the questions below.

In Jesus, how can the command to love each other be a new command when it's also an old one God's people have heard from the beginning?

In what way does loving others feel new and exciting to you, like stepping out of darkness and into light?

Verse 16 lists three temptations from the world: "the lust of the flesh, the lust of the eyes, and the pride of life." How do these keep you from loving other people? (Here *lust* means any misplaced desire, not necessarily a sexual one.)

✶✶✶✶✶

Now read aloud the article, "New-Command Living," taking turns by paragraph. Then discuss the questions that follow.

Lesson

ARTICLE

3

NEW-COMMAND LIVING

5 MINUTES

John sat with Jesus the night our Savior declared love to be the true mark of his disciples: "A new command I give you: Love one another. As I have loved you, so you must love one another. By this everyone will know that you are my disciples, if you love one another" (John 13:34–35).

The apostle captured his memory of that evening with this vivid description: "Having loved his own who were in the world, he loved them to the end" (John 13:1). Within twenty-four hours of giving his disciples the new command, Jesus went from getting low to wash their feet to being lifted onto a cross to cleanse their hearts. How could John and his friends possibly have imagined the death of Jesus would be the greatest expression of the love of Jesus?

During that evening, Jesus also told them, "Greater love has no one than this: to lay down one's life for one's friends" (John 15:13). What did that mean to them? Was it a call to follow Jesus in his humility and servant leadership? Yes, but it was so much more. To have their friend take the punishment for their sin was far beyond having him give an example to follow—a difference of light years, and the gospel.

After the resurrection, John and the others began to understand how Jesus is the Yes to every promise God has made. With the gift of the Holy Spirit, John's understanding of Jesus and his love kept expanding. And the resurrected Jesus had even more to share with John, recorded for us in the book of Revelation, which opens with a magnificent burst of adoration and praise to Jesus: "To him who loves us and has freed us from our sins by his blood" (1:5). Revelation continues with a series of visions, growing in grandeur, all pointing to the day when Jesus will return to consummate his great love for his bride at the wedding feast of the Lamb.

John's life was an answer to Paul's prayer in Ephesians: "I pray that you, being rooted and established in love, may have power, together with all the Lord's holy people, to grasp how wide and long and high and deep is the love of Christ, and to know this love that surpasses knowledge" (Ephesians 3:17–19).

By the time he wrote 1 John, the apostle was probably in his mid-eighties. But John continued his growth in gospel astonishment, and also in his love and service to others. The second half of the new command ("You must love one another") is the arena for celebrating the first half ("I have loved you"). We are to love each other in response to Jesus's love for us.

The aged apostle had been so indelibly impacted by the call to new-command living that he used the word *love* fifty-seven times in his gospel—more often than it's used in the other three gospels combined—and forty-six times in 1 John. Claiming to love an invisible God while disregarding one's very visible neighbors was a non sequitur for John. You can't be an unloving person when your whole life flows from love.

The false teachers' spiritual elitism and insider-outsider mentality stood against the relational culture created by the gospel. The false teachers presented more of an "everyone for themselves" spirituality. The gospel frees us for a lifestyle of servant love—service first unto Jesus, but also always for the benefit of our neighbors. Paul described the gospel-saturated life in these words: "Christ's love compels us, because we are convinced that one died for all, and therefore all died. And he died for all, that those who live should no longer live for themselves but for him who died for them and was raised again" (2 Corinthians 5:14–15).

Nothing is more compelling and transforming than the love of Christ—love *from* him and love *for* him. Every distortion of the gospel invariably leads to self-preoccupation and away from neighbor love. The distortion of legalism fuels fear, pride, shame, and self-righteousness: "Have I done enough? Am I good enough?" And the distortion of anti-law promotes self-fulfillment and personal aggrandizement over servant love and a missional lifestyle: "I'm not under the law, but grace. Don't start telling me what to do."

But the gospel enables us to find our greatest encouragement, comfort, and satisfaction in our relationship with Jesus. This frees us to love others—not by thinking less of ourselves, but by thinking of ourselves less often.

DISCUSSION *10 MINUTES*

What is the difference between the kind of humility that thinks less of yourself and the kind that thinks of yourself less often? How might it affect how you love others?

How have you, like John, grown in gospel astonishment and love for others as your life has progressed?

Lesson

3

EXERCISE

"WE LOVE BECAUSE . . ."

20 MINUTES

John's instruction to love others exists alongside repeated uses of the word *because*. God's love for you and your self-forgetful love for others must go together. To have one without the other is impossible.

To complete this exercise, you'll begin by working on your own. You'll identify a way you can love others, think about John's "because" statements in our Bible passage, and consider how they go together. When the group is ready, you'll discuss your results.

Step 1: Loving someone else. Think of a specific way you might be able to practice love toward someone else. Make it something that fits a "think of yourself less often" sort of humility. Also make it an idea that's appropriate to share, since you'll have a chance to talk about it at the end of the exercise. (You aren't agreeing to do it, just to talk about it.)

A way I could practice love toward someone else is _____

_____

_____.

Step 2: God's love for you. Now read through some of John's "because" statements and how they reflect God's love for you. Be thinking of how they might encourage you in your love for someone else.

Mission. "Because the darkness is passing and the true light is already shining" (v. 8). With the first coming of Jesus, everything changed. You belong to an era of fulfillment—one that sees the gospel advance against evil as angels watch in envious wonder, wishing they could be part of it like you are. Love is the badge of this kingdom and of your citizenship in heaven. What a thrill to join God's mission, marching forward in love!

Forgiveness. "Because your sins have been forgiven on account of his name" (v. 12). As you have been forgiven, you seek to forgive. Since God has fully accepted you in Christ, you work to welcome and accept others. Because you have a merciful and patient Father, you extend mercy and patience to others.

Fellowship. "Because you know him who is from the beginning" (v. 13). There is nothing more beautiful than God, and nothing more agelessly satisfying than the love that defines him. As you get to know him, you long to be an active part of that fellowship of love.

Victory. "Because you have overcome the evil one" (v. 13). Love is the victory dance of those rescued from the devil's love-suppressing clutches. As one released from evil, you are called to love others before the watching world—in the country and community where God has put you, and in the places he will send you. He is filling the earth with the knowledge of his glory, and you offer a preview of the coming world.

Adoption. "Because you know the Father" (v. 14). The security, affection, provision, companionship, and eternal approval you enjoy as a child of God free you to love others. You no longer scheme or worry about those needs. You are finally able to forget yourself and serve God and your neighbor.

Strength. "Because you are strong and the word of God lives in you" (v. 14). When love is hard, you still press on with confidence because you have the power of God himself living in you and through you. Every promise God has made lives in you also, giving you hope when love seems pointless or impossible.

Step 3: Putting it together. Consider how God's love for you might encourage, empower, or compel you in the specific love for someone else that you have in mind. Pick a few of John's "because" statements that seem particularly helpful. Be ready to discuss why you find them helpful.

A helpful "because" statement: _____

_____

Why it's helpful: _____

_____

A helpful "because" statement: _____

_____

Why it's helpful: _____

_____

Now share some of your results. Which of John's "because" statements might especially help you want to love others, and why? Were any of them new reasons to love that you hadn't considered before?

WRAP-UP AND PRAYER *10 MINUTES*

Love that puts self-interest aside is an attribute of God, and it comes from God. So if you want that kind of love, be sure to ask God for it as a part of your prayer time together.

Lesson

4

REMAINING IN CHRIST

BIG IDEA

The best way to do spiritual warfare is to be preoccupied with Jesus, not with his counterfeits or his competition.

BIBLE CONVERSATION *20 MINUTES*

This lesson's passage in 1 John includes the terms *last hour* and *antichrist*, which popular Christian culture often associates with the final moments just prior to Jesus's return. But be aware that the New Testament treats the entire period between Jesus's first and second comings as the last days. It is a redemptive epoch, not just a final few years. The last days began in John's time and have continued until our own, and are marked by a focus on Jesus and by constant attempts to oppose him. As for the antichrist, this is a much broader category than the final personification of evil in one figure. There is a long line of opponents who have attempted to dismiss and destroy anything related to Jesus, dating back to the false teachers John denounces in his letter.

The good news is that despite this opposition we have unbeatable resources in Christ. John explains that we don't have to run after new and "better" teaching, only hold to the gospel truth we already know. Have someone read **1 John 2:18–29**. Then discuss the questions below.

According to John, what are some ways true believers are different from those who are against Christ? Where do you see some of these differences today?

What kinds of seemingly higher or more intriguing teaching tempt people away from the gospel today?

In verses 24, 27, and 28, John tells his readers that the gospel they heard and God's anointing remains in them, and so they should remain in Jesus (some translations say "abides" or "continues"). What are some daily habits that help you remain in Jesus?

*****

Now read this lesson's article aloud, taking turns by paragraph. When you finish, discuss the questions at the end of the article.

Lesson

ARTICLE

ONE CHRIST, MANY ANTICHRISTS

5 MINUTES

The Screwtape Letters by C. S. Lewis was one of the first books I read as a young Christian in 1968. I am quite glad about that. It helped me develop a healthy perspective on the work of the devil and spiritual warfare just when I really needed it. Mine was a generation of sensational fearmongering. Some Christians demonized everything from sin to sinus infections to sunglasses. Sunglasses?

Yes, one evening in 1970, I was visiting a house-church gathering when one of the elders decided to pray for a young man wearing sunglasses. The meeting stopped while the elder proceeded to call out a "spirit of hate-light" from the taken-aback visitor. The elder explained he did this because no one would wear sunglasses to a house church unless they were resisting the light of the gospel. I have many more examples, but I'll stop with that one.

False teachers in every generation seek to lead believers astray. Therefore, we must listen to the Spirit's constant testimony about Jesus: "The Spirit himself testifies with our spirit that we are God's children" (Romans 8:16). We must do so with a view to the second coming of Jesus, whose return isn't meant to frighten us but fill us with joy and hope.

Enter *The Screwtape Letters*. With amazing insight, C. S. Lewis introduces us to the wiles and ways of our defeated foe—the roaring lion who sometimes presents himself as a cuddly kitten. Screwtape, a senior devil, writes to his novice nephew Wormwood about the fine art of sabotaging Christian faith. The object of their sabotage is a man (the "patient") who recently came to faith in Jesus (the "Enemy").

Screwtape coaches Wormwood in the skill of tempting the patient away from a love for God and back into a lifestyle of other obsessions and preoccupations. Sometimes the temptations are intended to increase religious zeal, not diminish it, because Lewis understood that self-righteousness can keep us away from the love of God just as easily as immorality and atheism can. Wormwood is congratulated for his successes and chastised when the patient begins attending church, falls in love with a believer, and is called to service in the War.

The Screwtape Letters came to mind as I was meditating on this lesson's passage in 1 John, which includes some of the most misunderstood truths of spiritual warfare. For example, when I say the word *antichrist*, or mention the topic of the last days, what comes to mind? Sadly, both have given rise to fanciful interpretations, unfounded speculation, and great consternation. To see how the devil himself exploits what the Bible says about these things, I've written a Screwtape letter of my own. I hope it will help us consider these topics in a more biblically-balanced and wisdom-fueling way.

> My dear Wormwood, we have a grand opportunity to create a bit of hysteria and havoc among the Enemy's creatures, our patients. We do some of our best work masquerading

as angels of light: encouraging niceness without grace, and religion without faith. Other times we are quite successful creating intellectual suspicions about our existence. If our patients believe there is no devil—well, we have a field day with that one.

However, it's hard to beat the effectiveness of fear for wilting our patient's trust and enjoyment of the Enemy. And when we can mix fear with religious arrogance and competition— need I say more? Here's my plan.

In their dastardly book, our patients are warned about the "spirit of antichrist," and "many antichrists" going forth into the world throughout history. Left unchecked, this advice sabotages our element of surprise. We work hard to lull our patients into mediocrity and spiritual passivity, but that book calls them to study our schemes and be on the alert. I hate it when they actually think and watch. But I love controversy and hysteria. So, let's do this:

Let's change the narrative. We'll import the myth that there will be only one antichrist, not many. If we sell this illusion, think of the fun we will have. Our patients, in every generation and place, will spend so much time arguing over the identity of the one antichrist that they won't be as preoccupied with their Christ. That's our most desirable outcome. The less our patients think about their Christ the better.

We'll get them to create charts, calendars, and conferences for revealing the identity of the antichrist, and details about the end of their world—including the actual day their Christ will come back. The more competition we can create between them, the better. We'll raise up big personalities with big egos to do our bidding.

Let's suggest to them specific politicians, religious leaders, and other personalities as the antichrist. That will lead to openly ridiculing each other's views and gossiping about each other. How delectable a scenario! It's always a good thing when our patients criticize, label, and dismiss each other, calling into question each other's orthodoxy (how I hate that word!). They will blame each other, more than us, for the mess in their world. I can hardly wait.

DISCUSSION *10 MINUTES*

Consider some of the *competition* to Christ today: both spiritual powers and powers or agendas in the world that are anti-Christ. How do you sometimes give these competitors more attention than you give Christ?

Now consider some of the *counterfeits* to Christ today: personalities, movements, or achievements that may be good or even Christian but fall short of being Christ himself. How do you sometimes place more hope in these counterfeits than you do in Christ?

Lesson

EXERCISE

HEAD AND HEART

20 MINUTES

A lifestyle of remaining in Jesus will include two practices mentioned by John. You might think of these as practices of the *head* and of the *heart*.

HEAD: Remaining in Jesus means "you know the truth" (v. 20). You learn correct teaching about Jesus and who he is, and you are committed to hold firmly to it.

HEART: Remaining in Jesus means "you have an anointing from the Holy One" (also v. 20). You treasure the Holy Spirit's work in your heart, and you seek the comfort, zeal for worship, and humble nearness to God that he gives.

Head and heart go together. Studying the truth naturally will convince you of the importance of a humble heart that loves God and others. And drawing close to God through the Spirit will lead you to study the Bible, because it is the Spirit's word to you. Still, it's common for daily communion with God to fluctuate or feel lopsided.

This exercise will help you think about your experience of remaining in Jesus. Work through it on your own, and then discuss the questions as a group. (NOTE: Be kind to yourself and others.

41

Although a diligent use of Bible study, worship, and prayer is important to nourish both head and heart, factors beyond your control also affect your communion with God. There is brokenness in both you and the world you live in: depression, physical and emotional conditions, or old habits and teachings engrained when you were younger. So as you strive for better *communion* with Jesus, keep your hope in your *union* with Jesus. Your quality of communion will be imperfect in this life, but a believer's union is secure and unchanging.)

Head-and-heart diagram. The experience of remaining in Christ can be pictured as two overlapping circles representing the head and the heart.

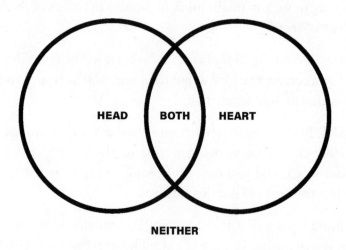

Think about your experience of remaining in Jesus. You might feel you fall within the "head" circle, or you might feel you fall within the "heart" circle. You might also feel you fall within both, or within neither. To help you think about where you fall, consider some common characteristics:

HEAD ONLY: You may have much information about Jesus but be dry in your heart. You are in danger of practicing dead orthodoxy. Judgmentalism and theological one-upmanship come easily. You may be quick to learn deeper truths, and even to teach them to others, but slow to pray, especially in private.

HEART ONLY: You may have much passion but be sloppy about the truth. You can be tossed around by faddish teaching or whatever feels right. You may confuse religious experience for the Spirit's presence. You may be quick to pray or to have a few Bible verses that inspire you, but you seldom study deeply.

BOTH: You grow up in the word and Spirit. Your expanding knowledge of God is matched by an increasing devotion to him. The combination leads you to forget yourself, so that life is no longer about your knowledge or your experience, but Christ's mission. You can love God and others.

Add yourself. With this in mind, add yourself to the head-and-heart diagram above. You might put in a stick figure or a dot to show where you most tend to fall. Or you might draw several figures or a circle to capture a range of experiences. Which part of the diagram do you mostly inhabit? Are you firmly in that area, or do you edge toward a second area? Have you recently moved from one area to another? Be creative (and honest) in putting yourself into the diagram.

When the group is ready, share and explain your results. How are you strong at remaining in Jesus, and where do you need for God to grow you more? If remaining (abiding) in Jesus is your goal, what does your life story look like? How can the group pray for you?

WRAP-UP AND PRAYER *10 MINUTES*

Pray for each other, that you would grow strong in Christ with both your head and your heart. If the exercise brought up specific needs, be sure to pray for those before you end your time together.

5

THE TRANSFORMING POWER OF HOPE

BIG IDEA

The more we see of God's love and our future, the more we will live each day for God's glory.

BIBLE CONVERSATION *20 MINUTES*

John has just finished writing about the importance of remaining in Jesus. Now, in a master-stroke of strategy, he's going to show us what beauty we will encounter there. Here in the middle of his letter, John invites us to stop, see, and savor a breathtaking gospel vista. He bids us slow down and drink in a vision that will empower us for the journey all the way home.

Have someone read **1 John 3:1–4:6** aloud, or have several readers take turns. As the passage is read, try to notice truths about Jesus that might give you hope. Then discuss the questions below.

John seems to want us to be astonished that God has made us his children. What about this truth astonishes you, and why?

Verse 16 says the hope we have in Jesus changes us: he laid down his life for us, so we lay down our lives for others. What other hope mentioned in this passage might change you, and how?

How can you love others not just "with words or speech but with actions and in truth" (v. 18)?

★★★★★

Now read this lesson's article. Take turns reading aloud by paragraph, and then discuss the questions at the end of the article.

OUR NEED FOR HOPE

5 MINUTES

Being slightly ADD, easily distracted, and having no internal compass, I get lost easily. I've learned to humble myself and ask for help. If I need to drive somewhere to meet you, don't tell me the first few turns. Start with what the final destination is close to, and then give me an overview of the whole route. Better yet, promise me I'll have cell coverage all the way from point A to point B, and I'll trust a phone app to get me there.

I love the forty-thousand-foot-view of things. I'm not bummed, but thrilled, when my wife gives me the storyline of a movie, and a general feel for the ending, before I've seen it. Sometimes all I need from her is, "Honey, trust me. It's a redemptive story. You're going to love it." Show me where the drama is heading, and there's a greater chance I will engage with the entire story.

I remember pastor Tim Keller saying he has read J. R. R. Tolkien's *The Lord of the Rings* trilogy more than twenty-five times. I tried, once. There were too many characters with odd names journeying through weird places. I just couldn't get engaged.

My good friend, Parke Brown, encouraged me to try entering Tolkien's world through the movie version of the trilogy—starting with the last movie. Parke knows me well. The great celebration in the court of Gondor, near the end of the movie, made me cry like a happy baby. Tolkien's insight into the story from which all great stories come absolutely undid me. Watching Frodo, Sam, and the other hobbits, surrounded by all kinds of creatures and beings, gathered in unity, joy, and peace—I'm weeping now, recounting a movie that so powerfully echoes the gospel.

I may not ever read *The Lord of the Rings*. But marinating in this lesson's text from 1 John has awakened within me the DNA of hope. We ache for redemption, reconciliation, and restoration. It's a part of being made in the image of God. And as believers, we are now pregnant with hope. Birth pangs are normal for those living between the resurrection and return of Jesus. Romans 8:23 says we "groan inwardly as we wait eagerly" for the redemption of the cosmos and for the entire family of God.

However, we often get tired of waiting. We get lost in the worries and weeds of our broken world. Can we risk hoping? Can we be certain of things unseen and outcomes the Bible promises that seem too good to be true? The God of all hope answers yes and fuels our hope. In the Bible, hope isn't a wistful instinct, a positive disposition, or a gut hunch. Hope is being head-informed about where God's story will end and heart-convinced that the journey there isn't in vain. Or, as I've come to describe it, hope is smelling the grass of the new earth so vividly that we continue our gospel gardening until Jesus returns.

John promises that on that day we will see Jesus as he is. It's hard to fathom everything included in that statement. We will see Jesus devoid of our stereotypes and cultural layering. We will see him no longer by faith or the through the blurred vision of our unbelief, but with our own glorified eyes.

Just how beautiful and loving is Jesus? How gentle and lowly, glorious and majestic? In the first chapter of Revelation, John's own vision of the glorified Jesus moved him to fall down in wonder, love, and praise. Those who see Jesus most unfiltered are most undone. No wonder John says "we shall be like him." Can you imagine yourself completely whole and wholly like Jesus: sinless and love-full, untemptable and not able to sin? Mind blown! Circuit board of my heart fried. Hope fueled with certainty of God's faithfulness.

John was a good shepherd and earnest evangelist. He understood that discipleship involves constantly drawing attention to Jesus and applying the implications of the gospel to our lives. He also knew that many people go to church before they come to Christ. So, throughout his letter, we hear echoes of this vital question: "Is this hope *yours*? Are you certain you know Jesus and have eternal life? On what basis do you call God your Father?"

As I write these words, the sights and smells of biblical hope have never been more precious and needful. It's the fall of 2020. I turned seventy this year just as the global virus COVID-19 began its relentless assault on my country, the United States. Well before COVID arrived, we were already as politically polarized, racially broken, and mean-spirited as I can remember—and so are many other parts of the world. We need hope not hype, and we need a constant refueling of that hope. God gives us both in the gospel.

DISCUSSION *10 MINUTES*

How does the knowledge that your life story has a heavenly ending change the way you live today?

The article says, "Those who see Jesus must unfiltered are most undone." What filters or false ideas keep you from seeing Jesus more clearly?

Lesson

EXERCISE

SEEING JESUS, GAINING HOPE
20 MINUTES

How great is our hope? Well, how great is Jesus? Notice that 1 John 3:3 carefully specifies that our hope is *in him*—meaning it is in Jesus, whom we shall see as he is. Our hope will be as strong as our connection to Jesus and our realization of his greatness.

For this exercise, you'll practice strengthening your hope by looking at Jesus. Begin by working on your own. Read through the descriptions of Jesus that come from our passage in 1 John. Especially notice those that may be different ways of describing Jesus than you typically use. Consider how they give you reasons to hope, and complete the sentences that follow the list. When the group is ready, finish by discussing the questions at the end of the exercise.

Jesus your brother. "Now we are children of God" (3:2). Jesus shares his Father with you. While some blessings must wait, John says this pinnacle of God's love—adoption as his son or daughter—is yours today. Your family status comes with multiple honors: your big brother makes certain you are protected, provided for, lovingly disciplined, assured of an inheritance, given a seat at the family table, and always heard in your Father's throne room.

Jesus your delight. "We shall see him as he is" (3:2). For John, the delight of knowing Jesus is his purity—how he is altogether righteous, beautiful, true, and loving. You have always longed to experience such a full and flawless person. Now he is yours to enjoy forever.

Jesus your purifier. "All who have this hope in him purify themselves" (3:3). Not content just to free you from the punishment of sin, Jesus is now freeing you from the power of sin. You are destined to become as lovely and as loving as Jesus, completely pure and holy. With such a glory-filled future ahead, you eagerly begin now to give yourself to the process of becoming like him.

Jesus the destroyer. "The reason the Son of God appeared was to destroy the devil's works" (3:8). Jesus defeated the devil at the cross, and will eradicate the devil forever at his return. You began life under the devil's power and condemnation, but he no longer owns you. The evil one and all who do his bidding are doomed— the Destroyer has arrived!

Jesus the sacrifice. "Jesus Christ laid down his life for us" (3:16). Jesus did so much more than merely make your salvation possible; he knows your name and died for you, personally. He who is perfectly pure spent his life resisting every sin and then died in your place, as if he were the one who had given in. Such is his mercy toward you, then and forever.

Jesus your rest. "We set our hearts at rest in his presence" (3:19). Don't listen to your heart's accusations; listen to Jesus. Your heart will discover the many ways you still sin, and will say you must fix yourself or live in despair. But Jesus says he has paid for your sin and taken your shame. Your need to perform is over. You rest in him, and obey as an expression of that rest.

Jesus your own flesh. "Jesus Christ has come in the flesh from God" (4:2). Jesus became human like you to share in suffering alongside you, die like you deserve, rise again to pave the way for your body to do the same, and ascend to heaven as a guarantee that you too will thrive forever in a heavenly home.

Jesus your strength. "The one who is in you is greater than the one who is in the world" (4:4). Not just metaphorically, but actually, Jesus lives inside of you by the Holy Spirit. You have unlimited strength to draw upon. It is power to resist "the spirit of falsehood" and all other pulls from the world, and a guarantee that your Father will complete his work in you.

Now use the descriptions above to complete the following sentences:

- _____ is a way of describing Jesus that is new to me or one I seldom consider.

- _____ is a way of describing Jesus that I find particularly astonishing.

- _____ is a way of describing Jesus that can give me hope in hard times in the world.

- _____ is a way of describing Jesus that can help me when I'm struggling to love others with real actions, tell about Jesus, or otherwise engage in mission.

When the group is ready, share some of your results. Explain why you chose the descriptions you did. How might more constant attention to these truths about Jesus affect how you live or how you love others? Try to give specific examples.

WRAP-UP AND PRAYER *10 MINUTES*

Your prayer time together might include praise for delightful things you've seen in Jesus. Also ask your Father for continued growth in hope and in the ability to love others with real actions.

Lesson

6

KNOWING AND RELYING ON GOD'S LOVE

BIG IDEA

The Christian life is a journey of growing in greater reliance of the love of God.

BIBLE CONVERSATION *20 MINUTES*

In John 4, we have one of the clearest definitions of God's love found anywhere in the Bible. It is the good news of how God sent his Son into the world to offer his life as an "atoning sacrifice" or "propitiation" for our sins. The Greek word is *hilasmos*, which means that when Jesus died on the cross he took the judgment for our sins. This means all our sins—past, present, and future. If you are a Christian, God's wrath (his perfect and holy reaction to your sin and evil) has been exhausted upon Jesus. Now God will never be to you a demanding Judge who punishes, only a loving Father who disciplines.

Those most alive to this love of God learn to rely on it to meet the demands of loving others well. We see it not as a chore, but as an honor and thrill, that God's love is made complete in us as we in turn love others. Have someone read **John 4:7–21** aloud, and then discuss the questions below.

Identify some key statements John makes about love. How might they affect the way you go about trying to love others?

Verse 16 says we both know and rely on the love of God. What can you do to know God's love? What can you do to rely on it?

Verse 18 mentions fear. What fears make it hard for you to love others, and why?

★★★★★

Now take turns reading the article aloud, switching readers at each paragraph break. When you finish, discuss the questions that follow the article.

Lesson

ARTICLE

A LIFE OF RELIANCE

5 MINUTES

Years ago, I was in a critical season. I was tired, conflicted, and angry. The juxtaposed whirlwinds of ministry and marriage had overwhelmed me. If I could have supported my family in any other way, I would have left vocational ministry.

At that critical time, my spiritual father, Jack Miller, powerfully modeled the difference between theoretical knowledge and personal reliance on God's love. Theological insight is important, and appreciation for God's love is quite nice, but *reliance* is how a believer lives. Reliance is the language of helplessness, risk, and trust. Our Father's love is for those who are bankrupt and hopeless. I qualified.

Jack had lived the story of desperation long before me. Along with suffering a heart attack in Uganda, he'd had a grapefruit-sized tumor in his abdomen and a live-in, schizophrenic mother-in-law. He had learned honesty, vulnerability, and joy amid suffering. He was able to model these to me, and it was instrumental in helping me own my desperation. I came to see that if there were one more beatitude in the Sermon on the Mount, it might very well be, "Blessed are the desperate, for only they can learn to rely on the love of God."

Of course, I had long known that reliance was important in *becoming* a Christian. I had started my walk with Jesus responding to a helpful, but insufficient, illustration of the Christian life. Perhaps you've heard it. It goes something like this:

How can we experience God's love for us in the gospel? It's like a highwire walker pushing a wheelbarrow across the rushing waters of Niagara Falls. We watch and admire his skill as he traverses across and back. But loud applause turns to quiet pause when then he turns and asks, "Who will get in the wheelbarrow and let me take you across?" Think of Jesus as the highwire walker, and the wheelbarrow as your act of faith. Will you trust Jesus to carry you from this world to the next? Will you get into the wheelbarrow?

That metaphor worked on me, and I "got into the wheelbarrow" and became a believer on March 7, 1968. Now, I have nothing but appreciation for the person who shared this illustration with me, and it's true that only Jesus can carry us from this world into the next. But a more accurate metaphor for becoming a Christian is a graveyard with us laying stone-cold dead in our caskets. How will we get out of *that* predicament? Our need isn't merely to get from point A to point B—from earth to heaven—but from death to life. "Because of his great love for us, God, who is rich in mercy, made us alive with Christ even when we were dead in transgressions—it is by grace you have been saved" (Ephesians 2:4–5). Those God saves by his grace are freed from their fear of death and have heaven as their secure inheritance.

But even more, I had to learn that reliance on Jesus isn't just about the beginning and end of the Christian life. It's for every day, dilemma, and demand in between. It's about *being* a Christian. God's love for us in Jesus takes on our wounds, enslavements, and idols. As John tells us, it expels fear. It also compels change.

Through the Spirit's work and my Father's pursuit, I have come to realize I'm not as free, whole, or healthy as God intends. I've needed more than a wheelbarrow ride. I need the spiritual power of resurrection, a perfect Father, and a tenacious Savior. Perhaps you noticed that I just referred to the whole Trinity. That's how needy I am, and how generous God is in the gospel. His love has proven reliance-worthy for my greatest needs, hardest seasons, and biggest hurts. Here is a partial list:

- From the start, I needed a new heart, complete forgiveness, and a perfect righteousness—needs met by the gospel the very nanosecond we come to faith in Christ. Until we see these three as our core needs, Jesus might feel important to us but not necessary and beautiful.

- I entered marriage emotionally frozen and "intimacy-deficient," as one of my counselors put it. Growth in God's grace, and reliance on his love, have freed me to get the help I need and learn to live from my heart. My marriage has never been healthier, and I actually walk very deeply with friends, not just superficially with reams of acquaintances.

- I suffered a major season of burnout and depression from ministry, and a significant aftershock. In his kindness, God met me at the intersection of my despair, hopelessness, and loneliness. The more we are alive to God's love, the less we look to our jobs, success, and people to fill us up.

- I resisted processing the childhood trauma of sexual abuse, and the death of my mom when I was eleven, until I was age fifty. By "the Father of compassion and the God of all comfort" (2 Corinthians 1:3), I have experienced much healing from my shame and from my inability and unwillingness to grieve my mom's death.

These are a few of my more painful, challenging stories. What about you? God uses a variety of moments, messes, and mentors to deepen our reliance on his love. Many of us have a photographic memory of such grace gifts. Others of us need to look back and discover how God wrote our stories with the ink of his grace, even when it felt otherwise. Will you risk a little vulnerability as you move on in this lesson? You have needs for which only the God of love and the love of God are sufficient.

DISCUSSION *15 MINUTES*

What moments, messes, or mentors has God used in your life to deepen your reliance on him?

What hurts or fears are you still trying to handle on your own or avoid addressing? How could you rely on God instead?

Lesson

EXERCISE

HE FIRST LOVED US

15 MINUTES

Even if we're very familiar with the line, "We love because he first loved us" (v. 19), it's easy to go through life as if the opposite were true. The devil accuses us. He wants us to get the order wrong. We start to feel as if God will only love us if we first prove we deserve it by how well we love others. But that self-first approach will never lead to true, Christlike love.

On your own. read through the descriptions in the chart below. They describe a life of "I need to love first" thinking and a life of "Jesus first loved me" thinking. Note some items that describe you, or show how God has helped you grow, or otherwise catch your attention. When everyone in the group has picked a few items they want to share, discuss the questions at the end of the exercise.

"I need to love first" thinking	"I know Jesus first loved me" thinking
When I hear stories about Jesus, I feel pressure to live up to his example.	When I hear stories about Jesus, I feel encouraged that I have him to trust.
When I fail to love others well, I feel judged.	When I fail to love others well, I expect my Father to lovingly correct me and to strengthen me so that I can love as he first loved me.

61

"I need to love first" thinking	"I know Jesus first loved me" thinking
Sometimes I'm naïve and think it's easy to love others (but this means settling for a weak love I can do in my own power).	I know Christlike love is hard—impossible if it depended on my own power.
Sometimes I despair of being able to love others and don't even bother trying, or I avoid noticing their needs.	Failure won't make me any less loved, so I'm willing to try even radical, difficult love.
I fear God's punishment. My actions that look loving are often just an attempt to avoid judgment.	Jesus took my punishment, so I'm free of fear. I'm able to practice authentic love like I've received from Jesus.
I fear looking like a bad Christian while others are watching, so sometimes I do acts of "love" to impress or look godly.	Knowing Jesus's perfect love, I have little need for approval from others. I'm free to truly love, without an agenda.
I seldom take time to explore God's love for me, so my heart is often just cold and unloving.	I am alive to the riches of God's grace. It makes me grateful and humble, which makes me able to love.
I often seem to run out of love. There's only so much loving I can do.	I know I have an endless supply of God's love. I turn to him to know his love better when loving gets hard or I run dry.
I tend to demonstrate my acts of love so others will approve of me. I'm frustrated if my love isn't noticed.	I'm eager to demonstrate Christ's gentleness, holiness, and love. I want him to be noticed and praised when I love others.
The mission of telling others about Jesus and witnessing to his kingdom is a duty I feel I must support to be a good Christian.	I love the mission of telling others about Jesus and witnessing to his kingdom. I want everyone to know the Jesus I know!
I seldom pray about the challenges of loving others.	My efforts to love others involve constant prayer. How else could I do it?
I have a nagging sense that I will only be saved to the degree that I can prove I love God and others well.	I am confident that I am saved to the degree that Jesus loves me—which is 100 percent.

When the group is ready, share some of your thoughts. Which pairs fit ways you have grown in the gospel, and which are ways you still need to grow or want to grow?

How would relying more on Jesus to handle your hurts and fears help you love better?

WRAP-UP AND PRAYER *10 MINUTES*

Even if it feels like you live much of the time on the left side of the chart in the exercise, God says that if you believe in Jesus, the right side of the chart is a more accurate description of who you truly are. It's true because Jesus has died for you and the Holy Spirit is at work in you. Pray that you would gain confidence that this is true of you, and that God would continue working in you to assure you of his love and to help you love others.

7

IT REALLY IS ALL ABOUT JESUS

BIG IDEA

It is impossible to make too much of the person and work of Jesus Christ.

BIBLE CONVERSATION *20 MINUTES*

The closing chapter of 1 John contains a discussion of "three that testify: the Spirit, the water and the blood" (5:7–8). Since John is writing about God's testimony of how Jesus is the Son of God, it is likely that water refers to Jesus's baptism, and blood refers to Jesus's death on the cross.

- Water: In his baptism by John the Baptist, Jesus publicly accepted his calling as the Messiah to be one of us and, as our representative, to fulfill the demands of righteousness for us. At that moment, God the Father spoke from heaven and testified that Jesus is his Son.

- Blood: In his death on the cross and his resurrection, Jesus became the righteous substitute who took the punishment for sin in our place and overcame the curse of death. In this,

Jesus himself speaks, declaring that all who trust him are fully and eternally forgiven and counted righteous.

- Spirit: In concert with the water and blood, the Holy Spirit testifies both in Scripture and in our hearts to the truth about Jesus. This means the Father, Son, and Holy Spirit are all declaring the good news about Jesus, so that we may have no doubts.

With this in mind, have someone read **1 John 5:1–12** aloud. Then discuss the following questions as a group:

In verses 1–5, what things distinguish true believers "born of God" from those who are not? What aspects of your being will be involved if you are a believer?

What does it mean that believers overcome the world (v. 4)?

Why is it important that our testimony about Jesus (what we say and believe about him) aligns with God's testimony about him?

*****

Now take turns by paragraph reading the article aloud. When you finish, discuss the questions.

OUR PROPHET, PRIEST, AND KING

5 MINUTES

As John winds down his letter, he unites three strands woven throughout—truth, love, and obedience. Each is a vital aspect of knowing God, and each drives us to the person and work of Jesus Christ. Knowing God is never merely a cognitive exercise. We are to love God with our whole being: "Love the Lord your God with all your heart and with all your soul and with all your mind and with all your strength" (Mark 12:30).

Only one person has ever kept this Great Commandment perfectly, and that's Jesus. Jesus fulfilled this commandment for us, and he is now fulfilling it in us. This is Jesus's work to do because, as John declares, "Jesus is the Christ." The Christ is the person who occupies the three primary offices God graciously gave his people in Old Testament times.

- Prophets, through whom God revealed his will and word
- Priests, through whom God mediated his mercy and grace
- Kings, through whom God exercised his just rule on earth

If we scroll forward a few years in John's life story, we see how everything he wrote about Jesus in his gospel and three epistles blossoms with kaleidoscopic wonder in the book of Revelation. There, John's opening greeting beautifully reveals Jesus as the prophet, priest, and king to which the history of redemption points. John calls Jesus "the faithful witness, the firstborn from the dead, and the ruler of the kings of the earth" (Revelation 1:5). Let's take a closer look at those three phrases, which celebrate Jesus in his threefold role—and his ten-thousand-fold glory.

JESUS OUR PROPHET

As the "faithful witness," Jesus is God's final word to us. The relationship between truth and trust is a critical part of life. Trustworthy information comes from trustworthy sources. For example, if I have a health concern, I want a doctor I can trust who will give me a proper diagnosis and the right course of care. Since I am not mechanical at all, the same is true for an auto mechanic.

How much more should we be glad for those we can trust to speak to us with authority about God, ourselves, and the world. John is saying we can completely trust Jesus. Jesus claimed to be the primary focus of the Old Testament: "These are the very Scriptures that testify about me" (John 5:39). And by his resurrection, Jesus has proven to be the one who fulfills the promises God made through the prophets.

As a religion major at the University of North Carolina, I wrestled a long time with Jesus's startling claim to be the truth, the giver of life, and the way to God. I romanced the notion that there might be many ways to God, and that spiritual sincerity is more important than theological clarity. I'm grateful to the campus minister who patiently helped me with my intellectual doubts so that now, fifty years later, I am much more at peace with the truth that Jesus is God's final word to us—and deeply grateful.

Many are just beginning to wrestle with questions about truth and certainty. Where are you in this journey, and how are your friends and children dealing with these kinds of questions? Let's not use our certainty to judge others, but as a foundation for kindness, listening, and serving—just like my campus minister did for me.

JESUS OUR PRIEST

As the "firstborn from the dead," Jesus is both the perfect sacrifice we need and the high priest for whom we long. Old Testament priests safeguarded the worship of God, overseeing the sacrifices central to Israel's worship. They also were charged with teaching God's law, offering mediation in civil matters, extending various expressions of pastoral care, and praying on behalf of the people.

The sacrifices were a testimony to both God's great holiness and his unparalleled generosity. God takes sin very seriously, and he takes his commitment to redeem a people for himself just as seriously. He wants us to come close, and his Priest provides the way into his presence.

John wants us to understand that Jesus didn't just oversee the sacrifice we need, he *was* the perfect sacrifice we must have. His death on the cross was once-and-for-all sufficient, and his resurrection is the guarantee that God has accepted Jesus's sacrifice for all who trust him. The writer of Hebrews says, "Day after day every priest stands and performs his religious duties; again and again he offers the same sacrifices, which can never take away sins. But when this priest had offered for all time one sacrifice for sins, he sat down at the right hand of God" (Hebrews 10:11–12).

The journey of getting this good news from my head to my heart has taken time, plus grace. I kept wanting to offer my own little sacrifices of religious devotion, self-denial, and promises to do more and try harder. Theologically, I believed Jesus did enough, but emotionally, it was hard to rest consistently in this good news. What about you? Are you currently enjoying the peace and certainty of Jesus's sacrifice on your behalf? What a gift!

And there's more. John also wants us to grow in our relationship with Jesus our Great High Priest. Jesus is always advocating and praying for us. He is our perfect righteousness before the Father, and he is perpetually kind and burden-bearing toward us. This caring kindness is how Jesus relates to you today—how he wants you to know him. As our Great High Priest, Jesus gives us a rest we can't find anywhere else.

JESUS OUR KING

As the "ruler of the kings of the earth," Jesus is the king we crave more than any other. John endured the narcissism of several Roman emperors and the evil of King Herod, so the bold declaration of Jesus's kingship was most precious to the aged apostle—as it has been to every generation of believers. Count me among that growing number.

I'm writing this at a time when I am greatly grieving the impact of broken governance in our world. My own country is politically divided, emotionally charged, and spiritually distracted. Perhaps because of those very things, my longings have been ignited and my hope supercharged for everything God has promised us in Jesus.

By his first and second comings, Jesus fulfills Isaiah's vision of a perfect king and everlasting kingdom: "For to us a child is born, to us a son is given, and the government will be on his shoulders.

And he will be called Wonderful Counselor, Mighty God, Everlasting Father, Prince of Peace. Of the greatness of his government and peace there will be no end. He will reign on David's throne and over his kingdom, establishing and upholding it with justice and righteousness from that time on and forever. The zeal of the LORD Almighty will accomplish this" (Isaiah 9:6–7).

John wants us to understand God is presently and zealously engaged in expanding Jesus's kingdom and peace. Things are not as they appear. As our reigning and returning King, Jesus is working in all things for our good, and all history is tied to his commitment to redeem his every-nation bride and eventually make all things new. Jesus's sovereignty is not just our creed, but our sanity.

How are we to love such a wonderful, merciful Savior? With respect to his three offices, here's how we might think about giving Jesus what he alone deserves and desires:

Prophet: We give Jesus our attention and conscience.

Priest: We give Jesus our sin, brokenness, and shame.

King: We give Jesus our adoration and obedience.

DISCUSSION *10 MINUTES*

What part of Jesus being your prophet most encourages you, and why?

What part of Jesus being your priest most encourages you, and why?

What part of Jesus being your king most encourages you, and why?

BURDEN-FREE OBEDIENCE

20 MINUTES

How can John say God's commands are not burdensome, as he does in verse 3? After all, we know that love is the greatest command, and to love the way Christ does is hard. It can feel like a burden. Yet woven throughout John's letter we find reasons why, for a gospel-believing Christian, it is not burdensome to obey God. This too is all about Jesus.

Work through this exercise on your own by reading the descriptions of how obeying might feel like a burden and why, in Christ, it actually is not. Where are you along the path of feeling free of each burden? When the group is ready, you'll share some of your results and discuss the questions at the end of the exercise.

The Burden of Worldliness
The world pressures you to live for self-fulfillment and fit into its mold.

Freedom from worldliness: Faith in Jesus means you have overcome the world. You are able to resist its squeeze and live a Christ-shaped life in the world.

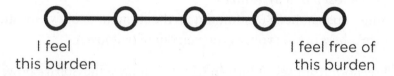

I feel
this burden

I feel free of
this burden

The Burden of Drudgery

The world tempts you with the idea that obeying God will be less enjoyable, less secure, or less comfortable than what you want to do.

<u>Freedom from drudgery:</u> Because God's commands are about love, and flow from your Father's love for you, they become a work of joy. Hard things are no burden if you love them.

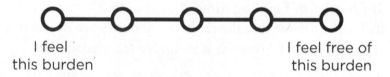

I feel
this burden

I feel free of
this burden

The Burden of Condemnation

Your failures to obey well, or to obey consistently, accuse and condemn you until you'd rather just ignore the commands that are hardest for you.

<u>Freedom from condemnation:</u> Christ has paid for your sin. He was condemned to assure your approval even when you fail. You are free to tackle even tough obedience without the shadow of judgment.

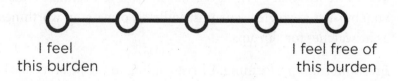

I feel
this burden

I feel free of
this burden

The Burden of Self-Effort

Your constant need to summon up the strength to obey God and love others breaks you, as you run out of willpower.

<u>Freedom from self-effort:</u> In Christ you have the Spirit's power. You don't summon your own strength or even summon him; he summons you to rely on him and follow as *he* leads the fight against your sin.

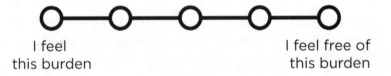

| I feel | I feel free of |
| this burden | this burden |

The Burden of Fighting Alone

It's lonely to wade into the challenge of obedience day after day, especially when no one else is around to see what you do.

<u>Freedom from fighting alone:</u> Christ has come in the flesh to be God with you, proving his commitment to be at your side, and giving you a family of fellow believers to battle beside you too. Are you aware of his constant presence?

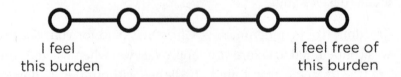

| I feel | I feel free of |
| this burden | this burden |

The Burden of Performing

The awareness that Christ is constantly with you actually adds to your burden, as you feel you must endlessly prove your worthiness as he watches for slip-ups.

<u>Freedom from performing:</u> Christ coming in the flesh means he knows how hard your struggle is and he sympathizes. He is your

gentle, compassionate, sinner-supporting Advocate. He is with you to help rather than to judge.

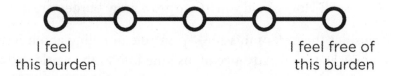

I feel
this burden

I feel free of
this burden

The Burden of Hopelessness

Your progress in obedience is frustratingly slow, or the world just seems to keep getting worse despite all your efforts.

Freedom from hopelessness: In Christ, your victory in the end is assured. And already today, every act of love you do is a participation in the forward march of Jesus's kingdom and a way to live out his triumph.

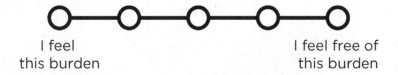

I feel
this burden

I feel free of
this burden

The Burden of Fixing a Broken World

You see unbelief, injustice, or suffering in our world, and feel it is up to you to fix this.

Freedom from fixing: Because Jesus is King of this world, you are *freed from fixing* what is wrong through your own power and effort, and are instead *freed to follow* his lead as he expands his kingdom.

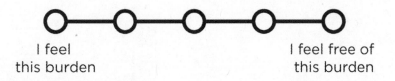

I feel
this burden

I feel free of
this burden

When everyone is ready, share some of your results. What burdens do you still feel when you work to obey God? What burdens has God released you from as you've come to understand and believe the gospel? How would you like to grow more burden-free?

Consider the task of mission—your role in telling about Jesus and joining in the advance of his kingdom in the world. What burdens get in the way of your service to Jesus? What freedoms are propelling you out to love others?

WRAP-UP AND PRAYER *10 MINUTES*

As part of your prayer time together, be sure to ask your Father to help you see and believe how his commands are not burdensome.

Lesson

8

THE CERTAINTY OF ETERNAL LIFE

BIG IDEA

God intends for us to have assurance about our salvation.

BIBLE CONVERSATION *20 MINUTES*

Our final passage from 1 John includes a reference to "a sin that leads to death." Most likely, John has in mind the false teachers who had infiltrated the church and their sin of promoting a different Jesus and different gospel. Theirs was the sin of being anti-Christ—refusing to accept the truth of who Jesus is or the salvation he freely offers, and instead pursuing their "higher knowledge" that supplanted faith and repentance.

In contrast, John wants true believers to be confident that salvation is theirs, freely and fully, through their faith in Jesus. They need no added achievements to enjoy the full wonders of God's love for them in Christ. Have someone read John's closing encouragements in **1 John 5:13–21**. Then discuss the questions below.

Notice the benefits this passage says are available to all "who believe in the name of the Son of God." Which ones do people (perhaps you) sometimes think are only for certain Christians who earn God's special favor? Explain.

How might you, as a group of believers, give prayer a greater role in overcoming sin and idols in your lives?

How might verses 19 and 20 encourage you to be involved in evangelism or missions?

✶✶✶✶✶

The article says more about our confidence in Christ. Take turns reading it aloud, switching readers at each paragraph break. Then discuss the questions that follow.

Lesson

ARTICLE

CAN WE REALLY KNOW?

5 MINUTES

"Of course you can't be sure about going to heaven. None of us can. That's why I asked for this appointment. I fear for your eternal soul, the people you're deceiving, and God's coming judgment on this big church."

We were sitting in the sanctuary of First Presbyterian Church, 300 North Cherry Street, Winston-Salem, North Carolina, though my guest was suggesting an impending address for me much farther south. Newly ordained, I was engaged in a one-sided conversation with "Jim," a traveling evangelist. He was kind, but doggedly certain I was promoting a hellish lie, and heading there myself.

Jim's target was pastors who teach it's possible for Christians to have assurance of eternal life—that is, to be certain that as soon as we draw our last breath we'll be welcomed by God into paradise. Jim warned me, "Nobody can know for sure they're going to heaven until they get there. But you can increase the possibility if you do these three things: Make sure you have confessed and repented of every sin you've ever committed. Be baptized by immersion by one of our leaders—three dunks, one for each member of the Trinity. And tithe to our church."

I got the impression that, for Jim, each of those big three carried equal saving merit. He didn't say much about Jesus other than stressing how we must work to be like him. When I asked him about Jesus's death on the cross, he said it was "important" but he couldn't really tell me why. When we parted ways, I was humbled that God had given me a heart to trust Jesus alone for my salvation. I also felt sadness for Jim who could quote so many Bible verses and have so much zeal, but make so little of Jesus.

Does my story raise questions for you, or perhaps ire and eyebrows? Maybe Jim represents what you've come to expect from all churches and Christians—criticism and judgment—so you respond with indifference or cynicism. Maybe you felt a tinge of anger if you were raised in legalism, never knowing if you'd done enough to please God. It doesn't take a lot to trigger painful memories of pastors, parents, and disciplers who put us under God's law but kept us strangers to his grace.

Or perhaps the issues of dying and heaven connect you to a story similar to mine. I grew up in a culture of an assumed gospel—assuming everyone was a Christian unless they consciously chose not to be. I was basically taught "justification by death." All you have to do to go to heaven is die. On the evening of my mom's death, I spent the night in the home of a neighbor who, when tucking me in, leaned in and whispered in my ear, "Your mom is in a much better place." I'll give her an A for caring, but that comment really didn't do much for my crushed, eleven-year-old heart.

And even if you've been taught well and comfortably identify as a Christian, you may have lingering doubts about eternal life and your acceptance into heaven. You believe Jesus died on the cross for you. You enjoy fellowshipping with other Christians, and you seek to honor God with your life. And yet you're still haunted by a bit of "He loves me; he loves me not."

It could be this whole study has led you to this very moment—to the spot where John says, "I write these things to you who believe in the name of the Son of God so that you may know that you have eternal life." As you look back on what John has said to you in his letter, hear the voice of a kind pastor pursuing your heart, not a prosecuting attorney looking to shame you.

First, John has highlighted the gravity of your condition and the grace of God's provision. It's humbling to realize there is nothing you can do to save yourself, but it's also quite freeing. John describes salvation as a new birth, not a new start. So his question isn't, "When did you invite Jesus into your heart?" but, "When did Jesus give you a new heart?" He guards against the error of reducing salvation to your own ability to muster up a "sinner's prayer" that's sincere enough. No lasting assurance will be found in your decision for Jesus, only in Jesus's perfect life for you. Simply trust the sinner's Savior.

Second, John has called you to keep trusting in Jesus's perfect righteousness. The only people who have eternal life are those who have a perfect righteousness. Believers are counted righteous in Christ the very moment they receive the gift of eternal life. Jesus's righteousness is put into the believer's account. This precious knowledge will keep you from falling into a "paralysis of analysis" with regard to your assurance. Salvation isn't based on the measure of your maturity, piety, or morality. Instead, John asks, "Whose record are you trusting for your standing before God? When did you come to rest in the righteousness that is by faith in Jesus?"

Third, John has emphasized the importance of fruit in your life without getting out the scales to count and weigh that fruit.

John is eager to highlight for you certain signs of your new life in Christ and evidence of the Spirit's work in you. This is an aspect of assurance that believers with a tender conscience can use to beat themselves up, or one that believers with a critical spirit can use to beat up other believers. But this side of assurance must never be isolated from the others. Always remember that you aren't saved to the degree you are like Christ, but to the degree you are in Christ. All who are in Christ have Christ in them, and it will show. Self-reflection is meant to deepen your love for Jesus, quicken your repentance, and drive you back to the riches of the gospel again and again. Every warning in Scripture is calculated to drive you to Jesus. Indeed, this is a most blessed vehicle of your assurance.

Lastly, John has stressed the corporate aspects of your salvation. Every *you* in 1 John is plural. Over and over, John stresses that your fellowship is with the Father, his Son, and one another. God uses his daughters and sons to strengthen and encourage his other children. He calls us to live as conduits of grace, sources of wisdom, and means of encouragement—continually calling one another back to gospel sanity and life in the Spirit. At a time when the ideology of individualism is peaking, and believers' disdain for the church is growing, 1 John highlights just how much we need each other. You are to live close to Jesus, and you cannot do that as Jesus intends if you choose a life of isolation. Our assurance grows—together—as we build each other up, pray with and for each other, and encourage one another all the more as the day of Jesus's return approaches.

Soon after I became a Christian, my first spiritual mentor encouraged me to start memorizing verses from the Bible. One of the first verses I committed to memory was 1 John 5:13, imprinting in me the Spirit's sworn statement that "you may know that you have eternal life." In colloquial-speak, "Boom!" The point is not that Jim was wrong and I was right. It's that God is this generous, even with you!

DISCUSSION *10 MINUTES*

How did your upbringing train you to think about heaven and hell, and how does that affect you today?

What have you learned from 1 John that has helped you know that you have eternal life?

EXERCISE

ASK ANYTHING
20 MINUTES

John says the confidence we have in God leads us to ask him for things, knowing that he hears us. As a wise Father, he has a wide range of good answers to our prayers: yes, no, not yet, "my grace is sufficient," and beyond-what-we-asked. And precisely because he is our Father, we want his will above our own. We learn his will in the Bible, and from it we pray boldly and humbly.

For this exercise, work on your own to create a brief prayer list by following the series of prompts below. Each prompt flows from a point John made in the last section of his letter. This means your list will focus on spiritual and kingdom-of-God needs, helping it align with your Father's will. When the group is ready, you'll share and discuss some items from your list. (Don't feel you have to come up with a request to fit every prompt. Just use the prompts to help you think of a few requests you especially want to make matters of prayer, perhaps including some things you don't often think to pray for.)

You might ask for spiritual growth and confidence. What do you need to grow closer to your Father and surer of him? What do you want to know? What do you want to believe more fully? What habits do you need to learn?

You might ask for spiritual growth or salvation for others. John says we should pray for our brothers and sisters who struggle with sin. Whom can you pray for (without being gossipy), and what would you like God to work in them? Who needs salvation? Who needs freedom from an addiction or sinful habit?

You might ask for release from the power of sin. John says God protects us from the power of evil, so pray against sin in your life or the lives of others. What sins need to bring greater conviction, so that you struggle against them? What other evils threaten you or others?

You might ask for the gospel to spread and God's kingdom to advance. John says the world is under the control of the evil one, but Jesus is reclaiming it. What places in the world need to hear and believe the gospel? Where might you and other believers show God's love? What might your role be in all this? What missionaries do you know, and how can you pray for their kingdom work?

You might ask for greater assurance of gospel truths. John says Jesus gives understanding and is our assurance. What do you want to understand better? What does Jesus give that you want to be surer about? What new confidence in God do you want to take into the next chapter of your life?

You might ask for victory over idols. John says to keep ourselves from idols, so start by praying for help. What gets your attention, affection, adoration, or allegiance ahead of Jesus? What do you trust more than you trust him? How can you give yourself more fully to Jesus, and live closer to him, so that these idols have less power over you?

When everyone is ready, share some items from your list. Why did you choose them? How can you continue to seek these things prayerfully, relying on the power and love of your Father to give what you ask?

WRAP-UP AND PRAYER *10 MINUTES*

Pray together for requests from the exercise. If this will be the last time your group meets, you might want to arrange for ongoing prayer partners or groups that will help you keep asking your Father for these blessings.

LEADER'S NOTES

These notes provide added thoughts and background information that relate especially to the Bible conversation sections of each lesson. The discussion leader should read these notes before the study begins, since they may help answer questions about the text that come up during discussion. Sometimes, the leader may want to refer the group to a point found here.

However, it is important that you not treat these notes as an easy way to look up the "right answer" to questions the group is meant to discuss. Most of the best insights will be those the group discovers on its own through reading and thinking about the text of 1 John. You will lose the value of taking time to look thoughtfully at the text if you are too quick to turn to these notes.

LESSON 1: MADE FOR INTIMACY WITH GOD

John describes both Jesus and the experience of eternal life in terms that go beyond the ways we tend to think. John's Christian fellowship (*koinonia*) implies a lot more than our contemporary use of the term, which often means little more than chit-chat around the coffee pot between church services. For John, to be a Christian is to be called into the deepest intimacy imaginable— the fellowship enjoyed by the Father, Son, and Holy Spirit before they even created our world.

Also, John is zealous to point out that this fellowship is for *every* believer, not just a spiritual elite. The gospel is personal but not private. Sin hasn't just alienated us from God, but also from one another. John will have much more to say about the corporate outworking of the love of God later in his letter.

The endpoint of John's introduction is joy. A Christian realizes that "the joy of the LORD is your strength" (Nehemiah 8:10). Joy is strength for glorifying and enjoying our God in every season of life. In Nehemiah's day, the Lord's joy empowered God's people to be faithful in the face of great opposition. The same was true in John's day, and it is just as true in ours.

By emphasizing joy, John was passing on the words and prayers he learned from Jesus decades earlier: "I have told you this so that my joy may be in you and that your joy may be complete" (John 15:11). John's letter will be filled with warnings because he is waging war against the greatest enemy of the gospel—the devil himself. "The thief comes only to steal and kill and destroy; I have come that they may have life, and have it to the full" (John 10:10). The devil is the consummate life destroyer and joy thief. Jesus is the quintessential life giver and joy fueler.

LESSON 2: JESUS'S LIFE FOR US AND IN US

There are many ways God is light: he is holy and pure, he has splendor and glory, and in contrast to the views of the Gnostics who thought knowledge of God was a hidden secret, he is all about openness and revealing. God wants to be seen and known, helps us see how to live, reveals his goodness, exposes our sin, and removes our shame so we can be open with each other.

The contrast between light and darkness is stark and all-important. In his gospel, John describes the incarnation of Jesus as true light breaking into the real darkness of mankind (see John 1:4–9). Fellowship with the Father means breaking free from the darkness of sin and death. We cannot even call God our Father until we have experienced this deliverance. In this way, Jesus doesn't just reveal our need, he also reveals God's provision. He is the "the light of life,"

God's way of doing for us what we could never do for ourselves: delivering us from darkness.

It is important that believers understand and embrace both Jesus's completed work for us and his ongoing work in us. Some group participants may be confused about the relationships between saving faith, justification, and sanctification, so the group leader should be well-prepared to explain this clearly and, if helpful, to refer to the notes that follow here:

The very moment we trust Jesus, we experience a once-and-for-all forgiveness for our sins. We are comprehensively forgiven and declared righteous by God. Jesus's righteousness is counted as ours (Romans 5:1–11; Galatians 2:16). The Bible calls this *justification*. This explains why John uses strong language in 1 John 1. Those claiming to be without sin are deceived about this non-negotiable part of the gospel. They are believers in name only and have no grounds to call God their Father. They must be called out, and called to Christ. When John mentions confession of sin, he is not speaking of a confession ritual but of the humble-heart attitudes of *repentance and faith*, whereby we admit our sin, turn from it, believe the truth about Jesus, and trust him to be our Savior.

But John is also addressing true believers who are already justified. Having a Savior means having not just a forgiver but also a purifier. John wants us to understand the process of becoming like Jesus, which theologians call *sanctification*. Every Christian has been perfectly forgiven, but no Christian has been perfected yet, and John's desire is to fuel our longing to be like Jesus. Truly justified believers work hard to learn and practice obedience to God—all the while relying on God and remembering that sanctification too is first of all his gracious work in us. Believers continue confessing, agreeing with their Father about their sin and their need for his ongoing, sanctifying work.

Yet as necessary as obedience is, it is never how we earn salvation or merit more of our Father's love. No one would suggest that our model in obedience, Jesus, earned more of the Father's love by his obedience. Rather, Jesus's obedience revealed and confirmed his love, trust, and enjoyment of his Father. The same will be true of us. When we live with the confidence that God has already credited Jesus's righteousness to us, our obedience becomes a sign of our life in Jesus (Colossians 3:1–4) and his life in us (Colossians 1:27).

LESSON 3: LIVING AS CHILDREN OF LIGHT

Throughout this lesson, be ready to affirm if necessary that we aren't saved to the degree we love well but to the degree we are in Christ, which is 100 percent. Yes, anyone in Christ will work hard at loving well. We must always ask, "What does the gospel look like in this relational setting? How am I to love this person as Jesus loves me?" But notice how John encourages the entire family with gospel affirmations. The motivation and means for growing in love are not shame, comparisons, or harsh exhortation. Follow John's lead, and remind your fellow believers who they are and what they have in Jesus.

In giving his "new command," John follows Jesus's summary of the Old Testament commands given in Matthew 22:36–40. We are to love God with our whole being, and love our neighbor as ourselves. The new command is a synthesis of both of these old commands.

It is also new because now it has been "seen in him and in you" (v. 8). Jesus is the perfect embodiment of loving God and neighbor, and believers who now live in union and communion with Jesus are a reflection of that perfect love. It is the righteous record we have before God, the guiding principle of our lives today (with new power to obey it), and the eternal destiny we await.

We should appreciate the newness of the era both we and John's readers inhabit. Old Testament prophets, and even the angels, were envious of those who would enjoy the fulfillment of the promises about Jesus (see 1 Peter 1:10–12). The light is now shining, John says, as we and others around the world come out of the kingdom of darkness and into the kingdom of Christ (Colossians 1:13). The old command to love is now in fuller bloom, more glorious than ever.

When John says not to love the world, he means we should not be ruled by the values, whims, and idols of the kingdom of darkness. Once again, he is faithfully passing on what he learned from Jesus, who prayed that in the world his disciples would be protected from the evil one (see John 17:13–18). Jesus asked not for our removal from the world but for our growth in his joy. As the Father sent Jesus into this world, so Jesus has sent us. All of history is tied to God's promise to redeem an every-nation bride for Jesus, and to finish making all things new through him. We are characters in, and carriers of, this grant story of redemption.

LESSON 4: REMAINING IN CHRIST

If your group wants evidence that the Bible refers to the entire period between Jesus's first and second comings as the last days, refer them to Hebrews 1:1–2 and Acts 2:15–18. These passages speak of how everything in the former days was leading up to Jesus (Luke 24:13–27, 44; John 5:39; 2 Corinthians 1:20), the promised gift of the Spirit, and the inauguration of God's messianic kingdom on earth (Isaiah 61:1–3; Ezekiel 36:26–27; 37:1–14). The last days are the days of fulfillment.

In contrast with the false teachers, true believers have "an anointing from the Holy One." Every true believer is regenerated, sealed, and indwelt by the Holy Spirit. As believers, this anointing remains forever, and it is connected eternally to the truth about Jesus. Our Christology—how we think about Jesus—is presently and eternally important. To deny Jesus is the Christ is to have no part in the Father.

Although the significance is hidden in our English translations, the word *you* also contains a key difference between true believers and false ones. The false teachers advocated an individualistic spirituality. But every *you* John uses here is plural—implying interpersonal engagement. True believers need each other all the time, especially during times of trial and stress or when false teaching comes at us. Both peer-to-peer and intergenerational discipleship are very important. Helping one another get the truths of the gospel deep into our hearts enables us to "remain in the Son and in the Father" (v. 24).

The word John uses for "remain" (*meno* in Greek) is one of his favorites. It means to "take up a permanent address" or "make this your home." In chapter 15 of John's gospel, Jesus uses the word repeatedly, teaching that we are to remain in him like branches remain in a vine—his words remaining in us, and us remaining in his love. A life of union and communion with Jesus is the best defense against everything the Bible means by the term *antichrist*. Daily communion with Jesus starts with a diligent use of the means of grace: reading God's Word, hearing it preached, seeing and tasting it in the Lord's Supper, and being faithful in prayer. Assure those in your group that God uses these practices to nourish our hearts. But take care not to suggest we should look to the quality of our daily communion with Jesus as our source of eternal hope. Daily communion with Jesus ebbs and flows, and sometimes suffers due to factors that have nothing to do with our discipline in seeking it. Our hope is the lasting and unchanging union we have with Christ by faith.

LESSON 5: THE TRANSFORMING POWER OF HOPE

John himself enjoyed the gift of hope-fueling, astonishing moments in his walk with Jesus. Among these, John was witness to Jesus's transfiguration (see Luke 9:28–36). This was literally a mountaintop experience. As Peter, James, and John watched, Jesus spoke with Moses and Elijah about his impending departure which he would "bring to fulfillment at Jerusalem." This was a reference to how Jesus's crucifixion and resurrection would fulfill everything promised in the Law and the Prophets.

As a man of hope, John bids us gaze with him upon the mountain God's love revealed in Jesus. John implores us to see—an admonition with the force of a *behold* with three exclamation marks. Don't glance; gape with mouth-open wonder! Don't take a selfie to post on Instagram. Get this picture written on your heart with the indelible ink of God's grace. Be dazzled and delighted.

The pinnacle of God's love is expressed in his adopting us to be his beloved daughters and sons. It is precisely because believers belong to the Father that the world hates us, as John mentions. Attacks and persecution aren't a sign of God abandoning us, but of our family status. This world is clueless about our God and his Son and is often ruthless toward his children. Jesus called this kind of persecution a mark of blessedness in Matthew 5:11. And our sonship guarantees a most glorious future—one not measured by streets of gold, but by the beauty of Jesus.

The ability to love others with Christlike love requires a gospel-powered transformation. Throughout this lesson's passage, John shows us how the indicatives of grace (who Jesus is and what he's done for us), always precede the imperatives of worship, love, and obedience. John takes several gospel truths he's already been teaching us and drives them deeper and deeper into our hearts. If we belong to Jesus, his grace and generosity will compel us to be compassionate and generous with our brothers and sisters in Christ. We who have been forgiven will forgive. We who have received mercy show mercy. Because we have freely received, we freely give. If we feel no compassion for those in need, and live a life of selfish hoarding, our claim to know the God of love is groundless and graceless.

All of this requires constant repentance from our natural tendency to love ourselves rather than God and others. Repentance will be a way of life for those saved by grace. As Jack Miller said, true believers don't have any less reason to repent than non-believers. Rather, we repent more quickly and more deeply.

LESSON 6: KNOWING AND RELYING ON GOD'S LOVE

John says, "Everyone who loves has been born of God" (v. 7). Love is the essential family-of-God likeness. Becoming a Christian isn't about making a decision, but about the absolute reliance of being born. Those who have been born of God this way take on the family likeness. We will love others because it's the way our family operates. We've been reborn into it, remade for it.

John says, "Since God so loved us, we also ought to love one another" (v. 10). God's love is measured and mediated by the gospel. In the same way, our love for others is measured by mercy—not giving what is deserved or earned, but full of forgiveness and grace. To make this happen, we draw on the fully reliable forgiveness and acceptance we have already received from God.

John says we know and rely on God's love because "he has given us of his Spirit" (v. 13). In the Greek, verse 16 can be translated "we know and rely on the love God has for us" or it could be rendered "the love God has *in* us." The double meaning is encouraging. It lets us know that the love of God both *for* us and *in* us is super-natural. *For* us, God has justified and adopted us, so we do not have to live with fear about what God thinks of us. *In* us, God is changing us by his Spirit and enabling us to grow in love. "God's love has been poured into our hearts through the Holy Spirit who has been given to us" (Romans 5:5). We must keep our eyes on Jesus, not on our own imperfect love.

John says love gives us "confidence on the day of judgment" (v. 17). The false teachers downplayed judgment, but John draws attention to it. Believers in Jesus can live with great confidence as we look toward the day of judgment. God's love has an expelling power. It doesn't politely nudge or shush fear away—it drives out fear. It is also a perfect love. The love God has for us in Jesus lacks nothing. It fully meets our need for forgiveness and righteousness. The more alive we are to these grace-riches, the less we will fear judgment—God's or anyone's—and the less we will be stuck living for the approval of people.

John says, "We love because he first loved us" (v. 19). This is the original supply-and-demand motif. God's love generates our love. We love *from* the love of God, not *for* it as if to earn it. God has called the church to be a show-and-tell of the coming of his king-dom. How we deal with our differences, brokenness, and rela-tional failures is a vital part of our discipleship. So what are we to do with the emotion of hate? We should redirect it toward our own sin and away from people—repenting quickly when we feel malice filling our hearts. We must wisely and redemptively deal with the ways we harm each other, especially within the body of Christ.

All who share the great hope of being made perfect in love (3:1–3) will demonstrate a fierce commitment to loving as Jesus loves us.

LESSON 7: IT REALLY IS ALL ABOUT JESUS

Be aware that some late Bible manuscripts include a reference to the Father, the Word, and the Holy Spirit in verse 7. Translations based on those manuscripts, such as the King James Version, will include this. This only adds support to the interpretation of the passage given in the lesson. If your group would like more evidence for how water, blood, and Spirit represent the triune God's testimony about Jesus, you might bring up some supporting passages:

- *Water:* See Matthew 3:13–17 for how God the Father spoke at Jesus's baptism (and how the Spirit was there in agreement, too), and for how being baptized was connected to Jesus's mission to fulfill God's righteous demands.

- *Blood:* The writer of Hebrews helps with this one, telling us in Hebrews 12:22–24 that the sprinkled blood of Jesus speaks. Through his blood, he declares salvation for all who believe. At the cross, Jesus's death gave powerful testimony as tombs were opened and even unbelievers could see that Jesus is the Son of God (see Matthew 27:51–54).

- *Spirit:* In John 14:26, Jesus told his disciples that a primary ministry of the Holy Spirit would be to testify about him—to remind them of everything Jesus taught. With the completion of God's revelation in the Bible, the Spirit now teaches us by helping us understand and believe what is written. We also have his subjective witness: "The Spirit himself testifies with our spirit that we are God's children" (Romans 8:16).

The Christian life involves our whole being. It requires right thinking: belief that Jesus is the Christ, the one who fulfills everything the Old Testament promises about the Messiah. It produces right emotions: love for the Father and Son and for all the adopted daughters and sons. It leads to right actions: an obedience to God's commands that is marked by faith and love, not pride or fear. It comes through faith, the core spiritual response we always must have to God. And it changes our relationship to everything and everyone around us. We become those who overcome the world and its patterns of living.

God's daughters and sons will overcome the world, but not with a boasting spirit. Instead, we will live to glorify God rather than serve worldly interests, and we will keep an attitude of redemptive hope. John specifies that we overcome through our faith in Jesus, the quintessential overcomer. Our focus is less on our "victorious Christian life" and more on the victorious Christ. Jesus taught his disciples, "In this world you will have trouble. But take heart! I have overcome the world" (John 16:33). He was referring to his impending death. He was so resolute about the cross and so certain of his resurrection that he spoke of overcoming the world as though it was already accomplished. Jesus overcame the world for us through his humble sacrifice, not an exercise of power.

No matter how profound, noble, or sincere our thoughts may be about Jesus, they are insufficient and dangerous unless they align with God's testimony. The entire Trinity beckons us to believe *into* Jesus, the source of physical and eternal life. That life makes us part of the whole new-creation order (the meaning of 2 Corinthians 5:21). The old order has passed, the new creation is here! To believe what the Bible says about Jesus is to be birthed into the eternal domain and reign of grace.

LESSON 8: THE CERTAINTY OF ETERNAL LIFE

Your group may have questions about "the sin that leads to death." Historically, the church has explained this, along with "anyone who speaks against the Holy Spirit will not be forgiven" (Matthew 12:32), as the sin of rejecting the Spirit's testimony about Jesus. That is why this sin is unpardonable. To die in a state of consciously rejecting the person and work of Jesus leads to death—eternal death. Of antichrists who preach against the truth about Jesus, Paul wrote, "But even if we or an angel from heaven should preach a gospel other than the one we preached to you, let them be under God's curse!" (Galatians 1:8). Neither John nor Paul is suggesting true believers can lose their salvation. But both are making it clear: whomever you are, be sure you receive salvation as it is given to us, fully and freely, through the person and work of Jesus.

Believing "in the name of God's Son" is John's way of telling us to make sure which Jesus we are believing in. Jesus's name includes everything the Bible declares to be true about his person and work. By using the name *Son of God*, John makes a clear distinction between the Jesus he preached and the lesser Jesus of the false teachers. Jesus is the Son, eternally one with the Father. He is God incarnate. He is Lord of all. He is Jesus, "because he will save his people from their sins" (Matthew 1:21). He is the Christ, the title given to the promised Messiah.

A true convert will have *saving faith*: you believe these truths about Jesus and put your hope in him alone as your Savior. With this will come *repentance*: you admit your sin and are sorry for it, and you change your approach to sin to become a person who fights against it. This means believers are marked by a change in their inner disposition, not by how much outward reform or learning they have achieved. The Gnostics rejected all of this.

True believers excel at receiving. Those who have eternal life most confidently and readily come to the throne of grace, where our Father rules all things. And as our life of worship, grace, and prayer deepens, so will our engagement with those around us. We won't just bring ourselves to the throne of grace, but others as well.

At first reading, verses 16 and 17 are two of the most difficult verses in 1 John to understand, but keep in mind John's original audience. The young churches in Asia Minor would have included strong believers, young believers, almost-believers (those who may already identify as Christians but actually have yet to be converted), and non-believers. Praying for "brothers and sisters" engaged in various degrees of sin means investing in the lives of all of these.

Some may also ask what John means by "anyone born of God does not continue to sin" in verse 18. As he has elsewhere, John is referring to sin as a life-defining characteristic, not individual instances of sin. He has just explained that there are both individual instances of sin (sin that does not lead to death) and the life-defining sin of rejecting Jesus as Savior (sin that leads to death). Now John confirms that Jesus, "the One who was born of God," safely keeps those who have received him, and that Satan cannot harm them. They rest securely in God's hands and their identity as a "saint" cannot be taken away or changed back to "sinner." It is in this sense of looking at the entirety of our salvation that believers do not continue to sin.

mission
propelled by good news

At Serge we believe that mission begins through the gospel of Jesus Christ bringing God's grace into the lives of believers. This good news also sustains and empowers us to cross nations and cultures to bring the gospel of grace to those whom God is calling to himself.

As a cross-denominational, reformed sending agency with more than two hundred missionaries and twenty-five teams in five continents, we are always looking for people who are ready to take the next step in sharing Christ through:

- **Short-term Teams:** One- to two-week trips oriented around serving overseas ministries while equipping the local church for mission
- **Internships:** Eight-week to nine-month opportunities to learn about missions through serving with our overseas ministry teams
- **Apprenticeships:** Intensive twelve- to twenty-four-month training and ministry opportunities for those discerning their call to cross-cultural ministry
- **Career:** One- to five-year appointments designed to nurture you for a lifetime of ministry

 Grace at the Fray   **Visit us online at: serge.org/mission**

newgrowthpress.com

spiritual renewal resources for you

Disciples who are motivated and empowered by grace to reach out to a broken world are handmade, not mass-produced. Serge intentionally grows disciples through curricula, discipleship experiences, and training programs.

Resources for Every Stage of Growth

Serge offers grace-based, gospel-centered studies for every stage of the Christian journey. Every level of our materials focuses on essential aspects of how the Spirit transforms and motivates us through the gospel of Jesus Christ.

- **101**: The Gospel-Centered Series
  Gospel-centered studies on Christian growth, community, work, parenting, and more
- **201**: The Gospel Transformation Series
  These studies go a step deeper into gospel transformation, involve homework and more in-depth Bible study
- **301**: The Sonship Course and Serge Individual Mentoring

Mentored Sonship

For more than twenty-five years Serge has been discipling ministry leaders around the world through our Sonship course to help them experience the freedom and joy of having the gospel transform every part of their lives. A personal discipler will help you apply what you are learning to the daily struggles and situations you face, as well as, model what a gospel-centered faith looks and feels like.

Discipler Training Course

Serge's Discipler Training Course helps you gain biblical understanding and practical wisdom you need to disciple others so they experience substantive, lasting growth in their lives. Available for on-site training or via distance learning, our training programs are ideal for ministry leaders, small group leaders or those seeking to grow in their ability to disciple effectively.

 Grace at the Fray   **Find more resources at serge.org**

newgrowthpress.com

resources and mentoring
for every stage of
growth

Every day around the world, Serge teams help people develop and deepen a living, breathing, growing relationship with Jesus. We help people connect with God in ways that are genuinely grace-motivated and increase desire and ability to reach out to others. No matter where you are along the way, we have a series that is right for you.

101: The Gospel-Centered Series

Our *Gospel-Centered* series is simple, deep, and transformative. Each *Gospel-Centered* lesson features an easy-to-read article and provides challenging discussion questions and application questions. Best of all, no outside preparation on the part of the participants is needed! They are perfect for small groups, those who are seeking to develop "gospel DNA" in their organizations and leaders, and contexts where people are still wrestling with what it means to follow Jesus.

201: The Gospel Transformation Series

Our *Gospel Transformation* studies take the themes introduced in our 101-level materials and expand and deepen them. Designed for those seeking to grow through directly studying Scripture, each *Gospel Transformation* lesson helps participants grow in the way they understand and experience God's grace. Ideal for small groups, individuals who are ready for more, and one-on-one mentoring, *Gospel Identity, Gospel Growth*, and *Gospel Love* provide substantive material, in easy-to-use, manageable sized studies.

The Sonship Course and Individual Mentoring from Serge

Developed for use with our own missionaries and used for over twenty-five years with thousands of Christian leaders in every corner of the world, Sonship sets the standard for whole-person, life transformation through the gospel. Designed to be used with a mentor or in groups ready for a high investment with each other, each lesson focuses on the type of "inductive heart study" that brings about change from the inside out.

 Grace at the Fray   **Visit us online at serge.org**

newgrowthpress.com